BETWEEN
ME & DAD

A JOURNEY THROUGH FORGIVENESS TO FREEDOM

CHARLES HOLT

Charles Holt Productions, LLC
Los Angeles, California

Published by Charles Holt Productions, LLC
8033 Sunset Boulevard
Suite 167
Los Angeles, CA 90046
213-309-2615
www.betweenmeanddad.com

Distributed by Charles Holt Productions, LLC
www.charlesholtproductions.com

Between Me and Dad
Charles Holt

Editor: Kuwana Haulsey
Book Cover and Interior Design: Pip Abrigo
Executive in Charge of Publication: Charles Holt

Printed in USA on recycled paper

ISBN: 978-0-615-97668-6

Acknowledgements

To my mother, my hero and best friend, who continues to hold us together. I thank you for always loving me without reservation and for giving me permission to be all that I came to be. To my brother, who embodied unconditional love towards my father, I am grateful for you. To my sister who made sure things were in order and of my dad's best interest. To Patdro Harris for seeing gifts and talents in me that I was blind to and who encouraged me to step out into faith; Dr. Michael Beckwith, who through one spoken word opened my soul up to remember who I am, and who continues to encourage me to continue on my path of truth; Rickie Byars Beckwith for singing the song of life and for steering me toward compassion; Dr. Lissa Sprinkles, my confidante and witness to that which is present, available, and possible; my soul brother, Dorian Baucum, who holds me in the light of all good, reminding me to embody deep listening. And to my friends who behold from the invisible: Carl Anderson who still shows me how to illuminate the stage; Freda Buford, who held my hand while I sang my first solo in church. To Lula Jordan Perry who prophetically spoke of things to come and the unfolding good that awaited me on my path to self-discovery. And to my ancestors, particularly my beloved grandmother, Wilhelmina, and to "grandpa", who continue to hold the high watch and the vision.

To my father, for teaching me how to live my life according to how I believe and not what others may say or believe about me, and for the charge to share all the good of my life with others so that we all can heal and be forever free.

I am Forever Grateful,

Charles Holt

Contents

"I Am" Produced by Ben Dowling

1. America the Beautiful
2. Tapping
3. I Am
4. Love's In Need
5. Summertime
6. Jesus Loves Me
7. A Place at the Table
8. Seasons of Love
9. In Your Eyes
10. Come Sunday

"Rushing Over Me" Produced by Ben Dowling & Karlton Taylor

1. Rolling River God
2. Narrative
3. Great Is Thy Faithfulness
4. Home
5. My Father's World
6. Narrative
7. God Bless The Child
8. I Forgive Me
9. Give Us This Day
10. My Funny Valentine
11. Use Me

Charles Holt Productions, LLC
www.charlesholtproductions.com

My father and I had a difficult relationship for most of my life. I blamed him for most of the unpleasant things that happened to me as I grew into adulthood. I blamed him for all the ways that I felt uncomfortable having to walk through the world. I also thought if anybody were to blame in my family it would be the head of the household, which is an indicator of how I really felt about him.

I thought my father was a king! And what I found out—after so many years of anger and pain and misunderstanding—is that he was a king! He just wasn't the kind of king that I thought he should have been.

All too often, we don't see that the men who sired us and raised us are kings. In other words, we don't see the spiritual truth of who they are. We see the exact opposite: all of the flaws and the shortcomings and unacceptable behaviors that cause us to judge them as insufficient. Unfortunately, that judgment often seeps into the other areas of our lives, poisoning our relationships with the people we love and even with ourselves.

Like millions of other men in our society, I grew up feeling the heartache of fatherlessness. The pain of abandonment and loss colored the way I viewed my self, the world, and the people around me for many, many years. As men, it can be painfully difficulty to hug one another or say, "I love you" to a close friend. We hold onto survival tactics from our father's generation even though the truth is that those tactics no longer serve us an individuals or a community.

But we can become square with our emotions, if we choose.

If not, all of the pent up emotion, which is seeking to be released, remains locked inside. It becomes concretized, weighing us down. Then we wonder why it sometimes seems so hard to get through life. We don't want to talk to each other about things that matter, because we're afraid that we'll be misunderstood. We believe no one will understand.

The healthier we become, the more willing we are to try to reach each other, and to tell the truth: We are not secure.

This book is about getting secure with who you are and your place in the world. It's about letting go of the outsider mentality and knowing that you belong. That your voice does matter. And that you're OK just as you are.

This book is a platform for men, particularly men of color, to let down our defenses and come to the table of civil communication. It is a platform for healing.

There are important things that only a man can give a child. Without that emotional, mental and spiritual guidance, boys tend to grow into manhood secretly feeling lost. Fatherlessness can look many different ways. Some fathers leave home, never to return again. Other fathers remain in the home, but check out mentally and emotionally. This was the situation in my case. My father lived in our home, but was emotionally unavailable. My mother did her best to be both parents for my siblings and me. In fact, I recall her saying to me, "I'm your mama and your daddy."

I was thirteen years old at the time. And I remember telling her, "No, you can't be him!"

Even then, I knew that my father had a specific purpose, even if it was just to show up with 1% out of the 100% that my mother gave us. But that 1% was equal to the other 99%. That's how important his role was.

There are qualities of tremendous value that fathers bring to a family environment. One of those qualities is order. Within the family there has to be order, and the father has the ability to set that order in motion. He carries the energy of the family, which indicates to his children that there is a way to successfully conduct themselves within the family dynamic. Fathers model how boys are to carry themselves in the world. Of course, mothers can do and say the same things. But the energy of the mother is different. It is equally necessary, certainly, but it is different from the energy that a father brings to bear for his children.

When men are properly nurtured, they grow to know certain things about themselves. They recognize the place inside, which holds the desire to provide for those who depend on them. They honor the desire within their hearts to be present, to be nurturing and loving toward their children and wives, and to know how to treat their wives in front of the children.

Men have their own unique ways of leading the pack. (This may step on some people's toes here, but I have to speak my truth.) In fact, men have an innate ability to lead. They have an innate ability to protect. They have an innate ability to serve. Men who know this find ways of being of service to the people around them. We also have an innate ability to create and sustain community. There is an innate ability in men to know how to call forth things into manifestation that is akin to a woman's incredible powers of creation. That is the truth of who we are. That is what little boys are instinctively seeking to emulate when they say, "I want to be just like my daddy!"

Of course, the same dynamic can happen in reverse. When

we grow up seeing the opposite, when we see men demeaning and destroying relationships, there's something that I call an inverted burster that takes the wind out of us. Sometimes, as children, we don't know what's happening. We only know that we love our fathers and want to be like them. Sometimes that desire—that sense of identification—is so powerful that we grow up and take on those same patterns as we get older, even if we hated them as children.

I grew up with the three strongest women I've ever known: my mother, my grandmother and my sister. But when my father stepped into the room there was something about my mother that would become softer, in a certain way, submissive. I don't say that to be demeaning in any sense. Again, my mother was strong and smart and capable. She held our household together. But if my father came home looking tired, the first thing my mother would say was, "What do you want?" If he said, "Can you get me a Coca-cola?" she was happy to get him one. She'd bring it back to him with a paper towel wrapped around it so his hands wouldn't get moist or cold from touching that bottle. I would look at this and I'd say to myself, "She respects that man!" And, because I identified with my father, the unconscious implication for me was that I was worthy of respect, too.

As children, we have all of our feelers out there looking for demonstrations. Children are not concerned about words after a while. They want to see if what you say is what they see in your behavior. Consciously or unconsciously, they seek to be just like what they see.

I wanted to be just like my daddy. I would pull his leg and hit him on his behind and do anything it took to get his attention.

But there also came a time when, after so many failed attempts at connection, ideas started coming into my mind like, "He doesn't like me. That's the reason he doesn't talk to me. He hates me. He won't play ball with me. He thinks I'm funny. Strange. Weird. That's the reason why he won't take me with him when he goes to see his friends."

When those thoughts began coming, they quickly morphed into false beliefs like: he doesn't care about me because there's something wrong and the wrong is in me. He doesn't want to be around me. The reflection then becomes one of self: what's wrong with me? Like so many others, I tried to find different things, people, or activities to validate me. Sports became that for me. But the whole thing behind being a standout sportsman was that I wanted to be good enough that I would one day hear my daddy say, "Oh boy! You can hit that ball!" But he never did. So I kept trying. I became a celebrated athlete because somewhere inside me I wanted to cross that goal line so I could say, "Look! I did it! Now what do you think?"

The pain and disappointment of expectation held me prisoner for many years of my life. I had to somehow get passed it. The strategies that I used to initiate that healing process are laid out in these pages. This book is meant to help others get past the same pain and disappointment, which seeks to define us and limit our limitless potential.

We are going to walk through the process of forgiving those who hurt or neglected or abandoned us. To forgive is to look at the situation from a different perspective, to listen before you leap, to really take a breath before you do anything else and ask yourself, where are my feelings coming from? For real?

Even if the end result is to agree to disagree, then at least we came and we talked about what fatherhood (and manhood) really means.

This is not a story about getting it all right. And though we (me and my father) did finally meet at a civil intersection before he made his transition from this earth plane, these pages bare more talk about the "not so good" times we had while he was here. It encapsulates a life-long course in finding the depth and meaning of universal principles as it related to my relationship with my dad, and therefore his relationship to me, his youngest child.

I had to dig deep to find peace, harmony, and joy in situations that were so painful that made it hard to do anything but pray for it to somehow go away, waving off feelings that were indescribable and almost impossible to explain to anyone. I muddied through disappointment after disappointment, filled with illusions in my mind of what I thought life was supposed to be. And yes, I spent years wrestling with relentless bouts of self-doubt and lack of self-esteem.

This is a story about all of those things and more. It spans the spectrum of emotion, time, and relationship, counting up the cost of a journey between a father and his son. In these pages stories and events are reflected upon to bring light to the good, the bad, and the awful experiences that ultimately made such a wonderful platform for discussion and healing. Great lessons were gained from each and every experience.

It is my hope that as we travel this healing journey together, we will continue to wake up and ask our self some difficult questions. As we make our way through this field of hurt, pain, harsh disappointment, misunderstanding and miscommunication, may we realize that we're being lead to an ocean of possibilities. We want to finally be able to lay those old burdens down and loose the shackles that have incarcerated our minds and thoughts, leaving our hearts encaged in despair. The resolve to claim our freedom is possible, but it must come through a subscription to self-discovery. It's an inside job that leads to exoneration, for the individual and for us all.

When I decided to print the page of forgiveness on my heart, instead of allowing the ink of past hurts and wounds to write more chapters of my life, a space opened up within me that housed everything I'd ever wanted. The biggest question in my mind remained: How do I get to THAT place?

As we learn to release unforgiveness and the stress of holding onto a desired outcome for certain situations, we begin to make choices from wisdom and not pain. We understand that our choices affect much more that just our own wellbeing. They have an effect on all those we come into contact with.

After years of searching and retrospect, I eventually stumbled upon the fact that my father was my greatest teacher at every step, especially when it was time to jump instead of walk. Everyone has those moments when it's time to make a quantum leap, when you're ready to move on to something greater and bigger. But you've got to leap over the ways of being that no longer serve you. At every juncture, my father, or something my father said, was there to hold my hand across to the other side.

Oftentimes, making these jumps didn't feel good. The pain and turmoil was indescribable. But instead of allowing my emotions to run my life, I had the opportunity to sit them on the table and ask, "Why are you here. What is it all about? Where does this come from?"

I'm not saying that we're going to get the answers to everything. Life is full of complexities, some of which we may never fully understand. But what we don't want are things that we cannot control running us and determining the quality of our lives and relationships.

This book offers every person reading it the opportunity to release the past to find their selves swimming in an ocean of new possibilities. We can then discover ways to use that newfound freedom as a jumping off point into something that is much greater. Even before my father released his body temple, I released him. Then I released myself. My forgiveness of my father was accompanied by compassion, for both of us.

Perhaps inside the pain of growing up without a loving father is the seed of our greatest strengths. But to activate that strength, we must to get to a place where we can at least recognize and acknowledge the pain for what it is. For such a long time, I thought that I could move far enough away from my father that the hurt couldn't reach me. I resolved to go where the disappointment could not catch me. I thought I could run down that football field fast enough to escape my heartbreak. But the sadness and disappointment were always at my heels, even when I wasn't consciously aware of the origins of my feelings.

Then it all finally caught up with me. But as I was broken open in my pain, I was also awakened to the truth that still I loved him so much. Because love for the father, is really love for one's self. This book is about releasing and learning self-love.

My relationship with my father was ultimately one of my

greatest pathways to self-discovery. The self-discovery was what brought me to love myself, to release him and to love him. Most relationships come into our lives for that purpose: so we can find out much more about ourselves.

The truths and principles that are covered in this book are universal, meaning that everyone can benefit from them. But the story is told through an African-American man's eyes. So a lot of the language in here, black men may recognize. But also, given the state of affairs in the African-American community, there are a lot of men, young and old, who have struggled with fatherlessness. Many have never met heir fathers, while others were forced to endure interactions with men who were vacant or abusive or neglectful or simply disconnected. Some fathers have already passed on. Some sons don't know whether their fathers are alive or dead. Oftentimes, we struggle through these experiences and, as a consequence, we say, "I'm going to be the man that he wasn't."

We work extremely hard to become settled within ourselves. But truth be told, anger and pain and resentment lurk just beneath the surface for the majority of men in this situation. Anger, as much as we try to curtail it, is a strong vibration that is not easily released. And if it's held for too long of a time without being looked at from a healthy perspective, it can explode in any situation. Anything can trigger it. In our desire to be more responsive than reactive, wiser than smarter or clever, it would behoove us to look at how our emotions run our lies. This is something that many men do not want to look at a great deal of the time, because we're not taught that emotions are powerful. We're taught that emotions are for women.

But the truth is that we can let go and not lose anything. That's where the gain is: in letting go. Many times people feel as though they need to hold onto their anger, otherwise the person that they are angry with will be "getting away with something."

But the truth is exactly the opposite: as we let go of our anger and pain, we not only release our fathers, we release our own frustrations and limitations. From there, anything is possible.

Chapter 1

THE BIG EVENT

The Power of Release

January 28, 2013
The Big Event

M y sister called me early on a Monday morning. I was on my way to workout and didn't hear my phone ring. While preparing to park my car, I saw the message alert on my cell phone and immediately called her back. She was at the hospital with dad and said she needed to speak with me about his condition.

My father had been diagnosed with end stage renal disease and, for the past seven years, he'd been on dialysis. Approaching 88 years of age, he had courageously managed his life with a condition that had worn his body down into an unimaginable state of exhaustion. It was a fight he couldn't win. Nevertheless, every Monday, Wednesday, and Friday he found strength to brave a 4 a.m. wake up call to get ready for a rigorous day at the clinic.

"They pull me so hard," he'd say, referring to the multiple-hour process of cleansing his blood. I never understood his pain, however the fact that he slept all day after a morning session was enough for me to realize that, though this was the way to keep him alive, it came at a costly toll to every part of his existence.

After hearing the sober urgency in my sister's voice, I parked my car and prepared myself to listen to what my she'd called to say.

She would never call this early unless it was a burning matter, I thought. My mind rushed straight to my parents. Mom, despite her aching, weathered knees, seemed stable in her health and wellbeing. Dad, on the other hand, had experienced a recent bout of severe pain in his lower back in addition to his other ailments. I had spoken with him over the phone and asked if he was ok. He assured me that he had outlasted storms before and that he would pass whatever kind of test this was, too. I rested in his confidence, thinking his condition was temporary and that he'd soon get better.

After a few days, however, his health worsened. My sister decided that he needed to be taken to the emergency room. Test results weren't good and he was admitted to the hospital. During this time he was not physically able to go for his treatments on dialysis. The plan was to get him into a rehabilitation facility so that he could become stable enough to resume treatment on dialysis. However, as one road to recovery opened, other issues with his health surfaced. By the time my sister called me, my father's life was hanging in the balances.

"His doctor said that it could be a matter of hours or, at most, a couple days before dad makes his transition."

Her words stunned me.

That doctor can't be talking about my dad, I thought. Maybe she needs to check him over again to make sure her diagnosis is accurate. The part of me that was in denial wasn't convinced that the man who had raised me and who I had known all the days of my life was leaving. I asked to speak to daddy. And, indeed, what I heard on the other end of the line was the voice of a man fading into his final hour. I listened for a remnant of what I'd always remembered and known, that unmistakable southern drawl, the way he was always able to express his vision for the future—dry, yet hopeful at the same time. It finally came. As I said goodbye I told him that I loved him and through a distorted, barely recognizable tone I heard him say, "Daddy loves you too, baby."

I was determined not to be overtaken by my emotions. But somewhere in that brief conversation, my father gave me permission to be fully present with my feelings. I wept. My sister returned to the phone and we both agreed that I should come home as soon as I was able. I made reservations to catch a flight from LA to Nashville the next morning.

I arrived home the day after speaking with my sister, not knowing what to expect. My mother was my main concern, and she seemed to be handling the situation with ease and calm. The lengthy flight from Los Angeles had spilled my arrival into the evening hours. The only meal that I'd had was a smoothie before boarding to Nashville, and I was starving as I stepped off the plane. I immediately jumped into my mother's car and headed to get some food. My plan was to get settled in for the night and head out the see dad at the hospital in the morning. However, as soon as I made a right turn out of the driveway, a voice instructed me to go see dad right away.

I found his room rather quickly, given that he'd been stationed in the palliative ward of the hospital. This section of the campus was where patients, like my father, could be relieved of suffering through hospice care. I found dad's nametag on the door to his room and entered. All of the lights were off. I was hesitant about turning anything on, given the fact that dad might have been asleep. As I approached his bed, I saw him rustling, seemingly in an attempt to get comfortable.

"Hey, daddy," I called. He paused for a minute, and then continued. "Hey, do you know who this is?"

"Yeah," he responded.

His voice was as I had remembered in the conversation with him the day before: course, deep, and vaguely recognizable. In an attempt to make sure that he knew that it was me, I asked him once again: "You know who this is, don't you daddy?"
This time he stopped and stared as if he was looking into some place far away.

"I can place the sound, but I can't place the face," he replied. Of course you can't place my face. You didn't even look at me, I thought.

As dad continued grappling with the sheets on his bed, I stood nearby wrestling with all the thoughts that had begun running through my mind. Episodes from our past began downloading. I replayed scenes from my childhood all the way up to the last time I saw him sitting at the dinner table waving at me as I left to travel back to LA after Thanksgiving. Like streaks of lightening, these visions were vivid, highlighting decades of memories.

I slipped out of the room to finally get something to eat. My thoughts amplified in my head as I walked the lengthy corridor to exit the building. I ate and then returned to my parents' home to be with family. I woke up the next day and got an early start to see dad. All the way to the hospital, I thought about the images that had been haunting me all night. My mind was inundated by messages from the past. Although they seemed to disappear in a flash, I knew that they held within them valuable information. The scenes spanned the emotional spectrum. The common denominator was that most of them contained painful episodes that had been too tough for me to digest in my earlier life. But now I noticed that, even in this full, vivid state of remembrance, the sting of yesterday's pain had far less effect on me. I engaged the stories, recalling many of the experiences as if they'd happened yesterday, but I was now able to allow them to fade into the present time and moment. Everything became about my dad.

During the next couple of days, dad became unable to respond to anything or anyone. I watched the nurses attempt to make him feel as comfortable as possible. The only time he made a sound—which sounded like a painful grunt—was when they repositioned him in bed. His breathing changed drastically from one day to another. The lapses between breaths became longer. Although he didn't exhibit any abnormal change in skin discoloration or swelling, the writing was on the wall. Dad's body was shutting down. My sister would comb his hair and make sure that he was presentable for visitors that came by. My brother, who had spent more time with dad than any of us, even came in to give him an encouraging rub on his hand and forehead. All I could do was watch and observe.

One evening before others had arrived, I went to be with dad. The doctor had told us that his vitals were stable, which was reassuring. She also mentioned that this behavior is in alignment with the process of a patient's final moments.

"It's common for them to rally before they expire," she said.

And rally, he did. Dad fought to the very end. With this in mind, my main concern became helping dad release without struggle. I believed that although he was seemingly incoherent, there was a part of him that could still communicate.

"It's okay to leave, daddy," I told him gently. "Everything is all right. We sure are gonna miss you. But I know that you're ready for your next adventure."

The following day, my sister, her son, and I had spent nearly the entire day at the hospital. As it became dark outside, I decided to go and be with my mother for the rest of the evening. My sister and my nephew took a dinner break with the intention of one last round to dad's room before returning to mom's house. Shortly after I arrived at mom's house the phone rang. It was my sister. My mother answered.

"Ok, I'll let them know," she said.

I saw the look on my mother's face as she responded. I knew what she was about to say.

"Your daddy's gone on. He's at rest now," she said.

I was stunned… for what reason I still don't know how to articulate. I knew, we all knew, that dad was making his transition. But the sting of that moment was overwhelming. Waiting in anticipation for that phone call was now over. All of the anxiety and growing sadness was now fading into the infallible beauty and truth of life–my dad's life eternal. That one particular moment in time, which seemed to linger in my mind as well as my body, is what I will remember for the rest of my life. On one hand, I was sad to the point of tears. I hated to see him go. I couldn't believe it. On the other hand, I felt relieved because he wouldn't have to stay in that condition any longer.

No more need to measure vitals or accumulate data or statistics. He had been released. Passed all his tests with flying colors, as he released his hold on this world and returned to his eternal self. Dad was free again.

To be able to release something or someone is an extremely powerful action that gives us the opportunity to discover more of ourselves. In our relationships, the power of release is evident as we continue to evolve. When we don't release things that no longer serve us, they become hindrances, whether those "things" are actually thoughts, environments, beliefs or even people. Holding onto things that have outgrown the container in which we've placed them in our minds is detrimental to our growth.

In relationships, we like to hold onto people. We don't want to let them go, so when something comes that changes the color of the relationship, we get defensive because we don't want to give up what is familiar, what we know about that person or our relationship to them. But it's inevitable: things change. Our time with the people in our lives comes to a close. Sometimes, we don't physically separate, but we realize that we must bring our relationship to the table and see how, if we chose to go on, the relationship can expand and continue to grow. Or if we chose to say its time for us to go our separate ways, how we can leave amicably.

What does all of this have to do with our fathers? What does this have to do with our relationships with the men in our lives who have reared us, and taught us (or not taught us, as the case may be) to step into our manhood?

Everything.

When I decided to forgive my father and attempt to reconstruct a new relationship with him, I had to release my beliefs about who I thought he was or what the old paradigm dictated for our relationship. For me to tie us both to my beliefs about him from the past, while still claiming that I wanted a new understanding of the man that I called "father," would never have worked. I had always felt that I was completely justified for feeling the way I felt about him (emotions ranging from disappointment to dislike to outright hate—or so I thought). His behavior had been wrong. I was right. Period.

I had to allow myself to move into a new thought, a new paradigm, in which I was able to let go of my positions and hurts. I got to entertain the possibility that perhaps I'd gotten it twisted all along. Either way, my old thoughts were in direct conflict with my new intentions. I had to give up the need to be right. Giving up the need to be right is part of the progression of life because everything and everybody is changing. Sometimes the change is quicker than others.

We're called to release something at every juncture of our lives up until death, which is the big release. When we hold onto the pain of our past, or to outdated beliefs about ourselves or others, things become unclear. Communication is misconstrued. If you're trying to transition into a whole new paradigm of thought, but you want to hold onto the theories and judgments that you think you can't live without, you're caught in an emotional and spiritual contradiction. Your beliefs about where you were are clashing with the truth of what you're moving towards. That creates a space for fogginess.

Old thoughts and beliefs that were born in pain, disappointment, sadness or fear, will not be conducive to the progression of the new thoughts, which are trying to create a new experience in your life. But once you transition into the new thought, it's possible that the old paradigm can be reframed. So, the perception changes.

When someone as loved and as irreplaceable as a father falls short in the eyes of a child, the aftermath is devastating. All too often, even as the boy grows, he continues to see his pain through his child eyes, rather than with the clear eyes of an adult. In this way, adult sons remain tied to the pain of what their fathers did or didn't do, the needs that went unmet and the questions that stayed unanswered. Releasing this pain and anger can seem like an impossible task, even if it is preventing us from creating healthy, fulfilling relationships in the present. The pain is what we know. The anger is what we know. The disappointment is what we know. Is it even possible for it to be any different?

It can be extremely difficult for people to give up what is known because we don't like change. We don't know how to change. But look around you. There are no such problems in nature. When it is the season for the trees to drop their leaves, the leaves simply fall away. Eventually, something more beautiful will take their place. It can be difficult for human beings to believe or trust that the natural order works exactly the same way in their own lives. Instead, the prevailing belief system is that you hold onto what you get until something better comes along. But when something better comes along, we don't even recognize it because we're not open to change.

In our society, we very often view change in terms of money. Men are particularly guilty of this, because we want to be providers. So when faced with the prospect of change, a common thought is: What will this change mean for my livelihood? Will I be able to maintain my standard of living (which often equals "my identity") if I embrace this change? That's why it's such a powerful thing for people when they get fired. When someone is fired it means they've been released, quite often kicking and scratching, from something they think they need. How different would it be if we realized that we were being released from something into something else greater? We don't really get that. The typical thoughts that run through someone's head in that situation is: I got fired... they got rid of me... they let me go. The connotation behind the phrase "let go" is that an individual is losing something. On the other hand, release says, I have the power to give this thing up or give it away, because it no longer serves me. We must relearn what change, and release, really signifies so that we don't resist its effects in any area of our lives. We must redefine the meaning of release. Think about it in these terms: Say that you're rushing to catch a flight and you've only got a certain amount of time to get to this new destination. You've packed everything and you're ready to go, but instead of rushing through the airport, you're just trotting along, putt-putting through the terminals while you drag these huge suitcases of stuff behind you. All of a sudden, you realize, "Do I really need all of this stuff that I'm carrying with me?" You take a survey of your inventory. You know you should get rid of some, or most of the stuff. But as you look over your belongings, you say, "I don't want to give that up. I like that. That has nostalgic value to it. I remember that! I'm not going to let that go." Everything has a meaning and a story behind it. But the fact still remains that the things you're trying to hold onto are the very things that are weighing you down. And that dead weight will cause you to miss your flight to your real destination.

When we look at release as being a process of letting something go in order to receive something greater, or as a progression into something that is new, then we can see release as an opportunity rather than a threat to our sense of self.
As relationships develop and unfold, there are the inevitable pains and betrayals that happen when people live and love together. A man's relationship to his father is no different. Unmet needs and expectations fester, creating an environment where the son feels justified in coming back and using the father's behavior as ammunition against him later. You did this and that justifies me not speaking to you!

So, the power of release is in allowing whatever you're holding the other person hostage over to be dissolved in your mind. This is where we begin to recreate and restructure ourselves, and our relationships. Instead of thinking about those negative actions from the past, we sit down and talk about them (if not with our fathers, then with another person we trust). This helps to release the congealed thoughts that we have in our minds that are not the truth and that are based on a circumstance or a situation that we've embellished.

One thing that release does is takes all of the emphasis off you and puts it on other people. Instead of looking at how you've been hurt, how you've been taken advantage of, how you're not getting enough of what you need, you look and say, "wow, how can I give them more? In the process of letting this person go, how can I give him the benefit of the doubt?" That is the power of release. In essence, you release your judgments so that the situation doesn't become all about you. It becomes about the people in your life who can benefit from your expanded perception of them.

How is holding onto the pain that you have inside affecting your everyday life? How is it affecting your relationships with the people who are important to you? If it's on your mind and has touched you to your core, then it's definitely going to spill into other relationships. To one degree or another, you will act out in response to that hurtful, painful relationship until you take definitive steps to heal and forgive. Sometimes we don't ask ourselves why we do what we do. Sometimes, when we get to the core of it, the truthful answer is, "I don't want to be like my daddy" or "I don't want to be like my daddy, but I can't seem to stop myself from doing the same thing."

What would it take for you to just be like you and not to strive to not be like him?

Trust me, I lived that life. And it haunted me.

Rather than staying mired in pain, let's use it to push us toward our goal of self-discovery. Pain has used us real good, so let's use it for a change. If pain has influenced your thoughts, feelings or actions, you must first get to the point where you can acknowledge the ways in which pain has run your life. Whether you admit to it or not, if you've had that much pain you've had pain run your life.

So, again, let's run pain for a little bit. Let's ask pain: Where'd you start? If you ask, somewhere inside of that you'll get the answer because the answer is nudging the question to get you to ask it in the first place. When you ask the question, make sure you write down any answers that come. Ask the pain: What did you mean to me then? What does you mean to me now? How have you affected my other relationships? How have you affected the way I feel about my self?

Now, you get the opportunity to acknowledge any areas in which you've acted and reacted toward others in your life from pain that was experienced long ago, which they had nothing to do with. Ask the question: Am I ready to give it up?

That's the million-dollar question. Some of us are not ready to give up our attachment to our pain. We want to hold onto it because it justifies us hating that person, our father, holding him hostage. Then ask, if I'm holding him hostage, if he's in prison incarcerated in my mind, where am I? Am I in prison with him?

Asking these types of questions is our introduction to self-counseling. We like other people to tell us things about ourselves. We want the friend, the brother, the pastor, the sophisticated instructor to give us revelations on who we are and what we know. But it's time to make a practice of understanding our own motivations and using that knowledge to invite peace and joy into our lives. The emotions that we take on become the things that we create and manifest and demonstrate.

Certainly we can ask, is peace possible for me? Is joy possible for my life? And if it is, what does it look like? What do I stand to gain from embracing peace and joy, rather than the pain? If it changes me, can it change my relationship? If I become forgiving of my father can it somehow allow my father to forgive himself? For me, it did. It's possible.

Of course, true release has in it the capacity to not hold onto anything. That means releasing expectation too. When we talk about the power of release, we're talking about something that serves as a tributary to self-discovery. So, as we move into the power of release, we know that it is guiding us yet further into the truth of who we are. We don't need to manipulate or concoct some kind of clever thing to get somebody to agree with us or act a certain way with us or say what we want to hear. We're just on our path. That's when we become demonstrations.

We don't just say, "Daddy, I forgive you." It's in our walk. It's in our hug. We stick to the release because that's what gets us on the way to self-discovery. It allows us to participate in the conversation that says, "I'm going to keep saying it because that's part of the truth of who I am. I don't care what he says!"

My father could have gone to his grave without telling me one time that he loved me. I was still going to tell him, "Love you daddy!" Because, I meant it. I released him. And releasing my father also meant that I wanted him to have the best life ever. Because, I was going to have mine.

Release continues to nurture encouragement. It's not easy to take the first step. But when you release what you've been holding, your heart opens. You've opened another portal into your own soul. That takes courage. Having the courage to release begat more courage and even greater release. You begin to let go of all manner of things that you've been holding onto. Then you begin to release you. You come to the understanding that you're all right with the parts of yourself that have been hindering you and you allow them to leave gracefully, gratefully and without judgment.

We're so powerful that if we get a glimpse of who and what we are, there's no stopping us. As we embrace ourselves, we can give from an inexhaustible place, understanding that there's more to us than we ever thought existed. We can say with conviction: I don't need nothing else to add to me or make me valid. I've got it all right here!

Chapter 2

TOTAL RECALL

The Power of Remembrance

G rowing into manhood without the support of a loving father figure can create emotional scars so deep that even acknowledging the memory of the pain can feel like a threat to our wellbeing. It becomes much easier to "forget" the heartbreak. We claim that it doesn't matter anymore. We don't care. We've gotten over it. We are so convincing that we sometimes even believe it ourselves. But this is almost never the truth. Seeking to escape or ignore the pain of growing up fatherless is the ego's attempt to protect itself, to banish our vulnerability or, at least, make it manageable.

But our experiences, no matter how painful, are doorways to some of our greatest lessons. As conscious adults, we get to re-frame our past. Our painful experiences no longer need to have the power to torment. We can call them what they are: challenges to overcome. Challenges create opportunities for us to continue to grow and not allow situations or people to gain control over us.

It's natural that, as we continue to grow and develop, certain experiences get shuffled to the back of our conscious mind. We stop thinking about them as often. Sometimes we forget what has occurred all together. But forgotten doesn't mean healed. All of a sudden, something will trigger an old thought, like the passing of my father brought thoughts, beliefs and emotions to the forefront of my mind that had been buried for years.

In the days that followed dad's passing, my life seemed to have been suspended as I tried to get a handle on the vivid images that kept flashing in my mind. Experiences kept resurfacing no matter how much I tried to shake them off. It was like watching a movie, frame by frame, and every frame included him, even the ones I'd hoped had been buried for good. Little did I know that this was just the beginning of what would become another lesson in healing and self-discovery - perhaps the biggest leap of faith that I would ever take in my life.

But in order to take that leap, I had to allow the memories to come. I had to stop fighting with my past. The significance of the power of remembrance was that the process created mental and emotional space, which had been unavailable to me before. For two weeks I journeyed through this process, first in getting home to Nashville and watching my father transition, and then being present for all of the logistics of the service and the burial, being reunited with family and friends. During that time, it felt like my life was suspended in the balances. All I could think about was my father. Memories just started downloading—things that I had experienced years and years before up to the present.

Of course, I started with some very painful and disappointing thoughts about actions, experiences and encounters that I had with my dad growing up. But I began to see the power of the remembrance because, through the sadness, I was able to stay aware of the fact that we had both grown into better, stronger men due to those experiences. Those things that had surfaced as sharp edges in my mind were now ready for me to once again reframe them. The memories were uncomfortable, but the more I sat in the discomfort, the less harsh and threatening the memories became.

Remembering gives us an opportunity to look at ourselves, where we are and where we've been, and encounter our own growth. We give ourselves another point of reference for the pain that we've experienced. We get to examine what that pain really meant for us at that time and to be honest about what still resonates with us. Most importantly, it gives us an opportunity to ask questions like, "Why is it still so painful?" "How, can I resolve it?" "How can I get past it this time?"

The point of empowerment is in finding healthy ways to traverse those sharp edges. We slowly start to find that we're able to swim in waters that were at one time too treacherous. We begin teaching ourselves how to navigate these chilling streams without losing our way. As I navigated the waters of my memory, I practiced allowing myself to float, to stay buoyant and calm in the face of turbulent emotions. The good and the bad flowed together, ultimately revealing a much more cohesive picture of my father, and of myself.

Early to bed and early to rise; that was my father's daily regimen. That's what I remember most about him. The time in between the two events is what made getting to know him so difficult. He never seemed to be at home; or at least home long enough for us to spend time together. He was a stickler about hard work. My father believed in honest living and order. Most of those principles were passed down through family traditions and cultural coding. I'm sure that many were also reinforced as a result of dad's time in the Army.

Subsequently, our house was full of rules. Many were unspoken, but rigorously maintained nonetheless. Along with the rules, came my dad's seeming emotional detachment. I hardly ever saw him smiling. Even with his best friends, a strong handshake was the extent of his physical offering. I never saw him hug anybody, including my mother. It wasn't until I was older that I realized the significance of simple celebrations like Valentine's Day. My father didn't celebrate what many would call sentimental holidays.

I never saw him bringing my mother flowers for any occasion. He wasn't keen on Christmas, grumbling that it was all about spending money you didn't have and creating heaps of debt. He had a particular dislike for money being spent on toys.

"He'll play with them today and you won't be able to find 'em in two weeks. It's a waste of money!" he'd shout.

My mother would spend the money despite his rant. He wouldn't even celebrate his own birthday. No cake, no ice cream. No birthdays, no anniversaries… it was a full sweep. If it weren't for my mother, we wouldn't have acknowledged any holiday – nor would we have known how to properly celebrate ourselves. His mind seemed fixated on what we couldn't do, instead of what we could.

Everything was always on his timing. A call to come inside after dark was a precise order. I would get caught up in a game of hide and go seek with neighbors and sometime forget the time. A fierce swat with his hat, as I passed him, was in order, even if I was just a few minutes late. Taking me to baseball practice had to be by his clock. According to him, if we were late in arriving to the field, he would be late for the date he had promised his friends. Once, when he was driving me somewhere, he informed me that I was using up his gas and I needed to start thinking about how I was going to contribute to his gas tank. The only way my five-year-old mind thought to respond was by laughing at his suggestion. It was totally preposterous to me. But one look at his face changed my tune. He was serious.

Another thing was that my father insisted on silence. Talking while at the dinner table was highly discouraged. Children or teenagers having conversations with elders, even if they were honest and respectful, were seen as disrespectful. If ever caught, you would be physically punished with lashings with switches or belts.

"A child should not be interested in grown folks business," he'd say.

The memories went on and on and on. Some days it felt like it would be too much to process. But I continued to let them come.

Part of the process of becoming all right with who we are (all parts of who we are) is allowing those things to reappear. They will, and should, come back to the mind and heart repeatedly. There's not a one-time deal on self-discovery. Growth and transcendence doesn't happen overnight. Circumstances and events may still trigger old attitudes toward people. Things that are triggers in your life will remain triggers until you can come to an agreement within yourself that the trigger isn't there to torment you. When you feel as though you're being tormented, the natural impulse is to run away. We want to do the exact opposite. We want to invite the memories in, so we can initiate the process of acceptance and reframing.

As we release the sting of past hurts and move toward having a new perspective, this is one of the key things to remember: do not run away when confronted with old pain! Don't think that something is wrong with you because you're having these impulses or feelings of sadness or disappointment or anger. Look at the triggers and ask yourself, why are they making me angry now? Something that happened so long ago (or even yesterday) why is it angering me still? Why is it lingering with me?

Rather than asking those types of questions, what we typically want to do is band- aid it. We put a Band-Aid on our sadness and anger by spewing it out at those around us. We lash out at others to get the feelings off our chest. We also go into what I call persistent habits, where we eat the pain away or drink the pain away or gamble the pain away or smoke the pain away or fight the pain away. We find any way we can to push the pain outside of ourselves. Actually, what the pain has come to do is to assist us in taking full power, not over just that situation, but over our life.

We aren't here to wallow in the pain, or to become inundated with our memories. It's true that sometimes the memories seem to come all at once. If you're not able to juggle and compartmentalize them and say, OK, I'll deal with you later, let me deal with this now, they can consume us. Then we begin to become someone else, not the person that we thought we could be or the person that we thought we were. What we want to do is acknowledge our pain, stand in our pain to see it for what it is. This is much different than wallowing in the pain. This can be a difficult balance to achieve because, for most of us, we've never been taught the tools for dealing with our internal struggles in healthy, proactive ways.

I know I was never taught these kinds of principles. My father's strictness combined with the absence of emotions was difficult for me to understand. On one hand, he ruled his household with such force. However he seemed incapable of showing his power through sensitivity or tenderness in any shape, form or fashion. Topics that brought laughter to the rest of the family didn't seem to resonate with him at all. Sometimes he'd have outbursts of laughter while watching The Flip Wilson Show and Sanford & Son with Red Foxx. Richard Pryor kept him in stitches. But absolutely nothing that I did could please him.

The only thing that we did as a family besides eat was watch television. We would pack into the tiny dining area right next to the kitchen and watch shows together. My father abhorred my favorite show growing up, Good Times. He would switch the television channel as soon as he heard the show's opening theme song. Perhaps the show's title, "Good Times," contradicted what he saw in a struggling black family—particularly a hard working father, who could barely make ends meet.

I think dad saw himself in that character, the ever-challenged "provider" of his household that couldn't seem to catch a brake. Perhaps he saw the story of a man who, at times, felt so frustrated with his surroundings that his impulse to dream of a better life was slowly beaten out of him by experience. The similarities were too painful for him. A reminder of what he had experienced all of his life was now spilling into the only place he deemed as a refuge. Perhaps the only place he felt like he was at peace in the world.

I often wonder how it was for him raising a son like me. I was a child of great expression and ambition. It must have been difficult negotiating his way with me. He was a man whose life was forever altered by the unimaginable tragedy of war and, perhaps even worse, returning to a society that could not encourage a healthy transition back into normal life.

My father kept his emotions sealed up inside him for most of his life. He would agree to laugh…sometimes. Crying, on the other hand, was out of the question. I once asked him how he responded to seeing his friends die while serving in the war.

"Most of us, my self included, were too numb to cry", he replied. "Crying was a sign of weakness, and there was no room for that in the Army. No room at all."

"But you're not in the Army any more," I thought.

For my father, there was no difference.

Living with someone who had so effectively numbed his emotions was devastating for me when I was young. I never knew how to connect with him. As a child I didn't have sports heroes. I admired certain athletes, but unlike most of my friends, I didn't desire to be like any of them. I had coaches that I looked up to. My junior high track coach, Fred Hill, had the greatest influence in my life as a young track star.

"You have the ability to be a world class sprinter, Charles," he'd told me.

My schoolteachers were powerful demonstrations of excellence in my life. They encouraged in my progress as a student consistently. My mother and grandmother were the backbone of my learning and development. My sister encouraged me to learn to count to one hundred in Spanish.

All of these people made it possible for me to be the person that I am today. But without my father's input, there was still a void that for years nothing in the world could fill.

Growing up, I remember carefully watching my dad make his way around our house. He never moved slowly, always dashing from one room to another. His face had a look of focus, his eyes concentrated on the picture that he had created in his head. He'd get dressed, eat a bit of breakfast, and then out the door he'd go. My eager eyes would follow him until he disappeared around the corner.

"See you later, daddy," I called out to him every morning.

"Yeah," he'd respond.

He would usually return in time for dinner. He had his favorite place to sit at the table, and he was the only one that sat there. He'd roll up his sleeves, put both elbows on the table, and dig in. I would follow his lead. I remember watching him when I was around four-years-old and trying to imitate him. At that age, I could barely reach the table. My arms were too short to match the arm span that he had, but I sure tried. I watched him eat, I watched him sleep. I'd even watch as he stood over the urinal. I took that instruction as well. I wanted to match everything he did. I wanted to be just like him.

Back in those days, my mother would take me with her to the Laundromat down the street. After she'd separate the clothes she'd designate me to make sure that the pockets were clear of clutter and change. This was my favorite chore. My older brother was notorious for leaving change in his jeans. In addition to the loose coins, every now and then I would find a few dollar bills as well. Out of three or four pair, I would accumulate enough money to supply a weeks' worth of candy and gum.

Dad on the other hand, seldom if ever left change in his pockets. He had a glass jar that sat on a small, square table next to the foot of his bed that collected his pennies, dimes, nickels, and quarters. Nevertheless, I searched his pants with a keen eye as well. I was interested in my father's clothes. I was fascinated with the size of his wardrobe, hoping that one day I, too, would be able to wear what I termed as "grown up" clothes. Before helping mom stuff the clothes into the washing machine, I would hold dad's pants up – waist to waist. I marveled at how much longer his were than mine. I'm going to be able to wear the same kind of pants he wears one day, I thought. I did the same with his shirts. I would drape his t-shirts over my "super man" chest and shoulders, and walk around pretending that I was as big as he was. I desperately wanted to reach out to my father, but I never knew how. He kept his emotions locked away deep inside, where they seemed impossible to reach.

Men, especially in the western world, use numbness as a tool for dealing with our emotions. Numbness is just an extension of what many would call normal. We aren't taught to tap in to our sensitive side. We're taught to stay away from emotions like crying, hugging even. We're told, "Don't you ever let another man see you cry. That's a sign of weakness." We've held onto those social codes for such a long time that it's desensitized us to becoming what the real normal is, which is sensitive, caring, nurturing. Most people don't use those adjectives to describe men, only women. Even I recognized where I had taken on those beliefs. I recall saying, on many occasions, "Oh my mother's very nurturing." But I'd never have thought of my father or the other men in my life as being nurturing.

We get caught in a web of social coding and perhaps at one time, those codes were of service to the individuals who employed them. For example, my father once told me that if you wanted to be in the army, there were two things that you didn't do: you didn't let them see you cry and you didn't let them see that you were weak, or else it would cause a ripple effect around you. People wouldn't feel that they could trust you in battle.

But, once again, when he got out of the army that stuck with him. So the integration back into society from his standpoint was full of stumbles. In talking about his adjustment back into mainstream society, my father often said, "I just need to keep this armor on so I can function in this place."

You don't have to be a soldier to experience that kind of emotional numbness. Many men still carry around these old cultural codes, because our society can still feel like a battlefield. It may not be a war like World War II, where my father fought. But in the minds of African-American men, our battles are just as real. We're in the war of survival. It's so easy to act defensive, rather than being vulnerable. It's hard to commit to investigating one's emotional side and exploring the pathway to loving oneself if a man is constantly on the defensive, believing there's a predator on the loose at every turn. Sometimes we fear that if we're kind to someone else, they'll see it as a weakness.

There is a very fine line that we walk. One person's concept of a healthy way of living may be totally different than another person's concept. And that's fine. But we must not acquiesce to living our lives inside the hard shell of self-protection. Bit by bit, as we strip away the armor, we reach a point of sensitivity where we can then become agents of transformation for ourselves and for others.

We all have our own individual ways of navigating the waters of pain and disappointment. But everybody has one thing in common, even if they say they don't: we all have something that is valuable and important to us. If we start investigating what's important to each individual, somewhere in there we'll find the opportunity to take the microscope off of self, and put it on someone else that we care deeply about. Numbness tricks us into thinking that we don't care deeply about the others in our lives. We don't recognize that there are soft places in that hard ground that, once you feel around and find it, may provide an opportunity to start planting seeds of growth there.

We must ask ourselves: How do we want to experience life here as we go forward? Do we want to live from a place of feeling incarcerated? When we numb our emotions, we become incarcerated in our minds, because numbness takes us away from the scope of possibility, of things becoming better. We go into our shell and say, "Pain doesn't exist! It's not true. Go away pain!"

Putting down the armor and choosing to stand in the pain means confronting the subconscious fear that the pain is so deep that it can be annihilating. Remember, we must stand in our pain long enough to gain strength and perspective and wisdom before moving on. But standing in the pain is a show of being vulnerable, you might add. And yes, I agree one hundred percent. However, we should remember that our greatest growth comes as a result of our being vulnerable rather than holding on to the misconception of being "strong." Go to the source of pain. Figure out where it started, when you began drifting further and further away from someone you desperately wanted to be closer to. One of the things that I discovered on my personal journey is that, when something happens in our minds, we embellish it and make it mean something much bigger than it is.

I recall my father saying that he didn't want to play baseball with me because he promised his friends that he was going to be with them and he wanted to keep his promise. But I interpreted it as, "He doesn't want to play with me. He doesn't like me. He doesn't want to be around me."

Growing up, playing baseball was my thing. Before I began playing for an organized team, I would grab one of my father's hats and pretend I was a famous baseball player like George Foster of the Cincinnati Reds. Dad had a thing for baseball caps. Very seldom was he seen without a hat on. He didn't own but a few, but he guarded them like he guarded his food. I thought the way he wore it was the coolest thing in the world. The hats always seemed to fit his head just right. Before I started playing baseball at the age of five, I wasn't allowed to wear hats in the house. Now that I had a reason, began wearing my baseball cap nearly everywhere I went too. I would adjust the back so that it'd fit my head like dad's fit his. The hat's bill would sit just above his eye line, making his hazelnut-colored eyes the first thing you'd see when you looked at him. Took me some time to get it right for my head, but I finally broke it in after putting it into the coils on the bottom of the exposed box spring of my bunk bed.

As I stated before, my father was a king to me. I wanted to be just like him. I wanted to walk like him. I wanted to talk like him. I wanted to eat like him. I wanted to sleep like him, on the same side of the bed. I believe that is common among little boys. They want to be just like their daddies. Some fathers continue to hold onto survival tactics that would not lend themselves to be vulnerable, not even to their children. It creates in the child a wall of emotional detachment combined with the physical need for closeness and interaction with their primary male caregiver.

I wanted my father to hug me, kiss me and put his hand on my head, which was a sign of knighthood to me. Just the mere touch of a king gave me so much self-esteem and self-worth and confidence. But a lack of it also had the opposite effect. Why doesn't my dad hug me? I wondered. Why doesn't my dad kiss me? Those negative effects continued to grow. For my entire life, I wanted my father's approval. But, like the warrior who couldn't show weakness without risking death, my father never revealed his heart.

By the time I'd graduated grammar school, I had given up on all of my expectations of my dad, believing them to be useless. I began to learn to make myself numb to the pain. My father became an illusion in my eyes. His existence in my life was non-existent. It worked for a while, but ultimately my inner desire to be accepted and loved by him was too strong.

Little boys intuitively expect reciprocity from their fathers. They expect their dads to be as proud of them as they are of their fathers. Because they love their fathers unconditionally, they expect to be shown love the same way in return.

Spiritual principles teach us that expectation is the quickest route to disappointment. We don't do things because we expect a certain response from a certain individual; we do things because we know them to be the right thing to do, and we trust and accept that our good will return to us in the best way at the best time.

When we look back and remember our childhoods, most of us can pinpoint specific moments when our father didn't do something he said he was going to do or we expected him to be there and he wasn't. As an adult, I can look back and ask myself what my father's past actions have meant for my life? What is the power of reciprocity? What is the power of being acknowledged in that way? Adults who can look back on their childhoods with a sense of having been valued and acknowledged and secure tend to access a level of confidence and self worth that is generated from that experience of life. It implies that we're cared about. If we have not had that experience, we can now generate it for ourselves.

Part of that process is to shift our perspective. We may decide to look at the other individual and what he may have had going on in his life at that time. To do so takes the focus off the lack of reciprocity. Instead, it places the focus on the value of the invitation to extend one's heart to someone else.

I didn't understand this as a young man. My dreams of walking in my father's footsteps took a drastic turn. After a while, I loathed the very sight of him. The journey was interesting and yet profoundly disturbing.

My behavior often challenged my dad's standards and way of being. I chose freedom at every turn: freedom of verbal expression, freedom to dance, freedom to excel in the classroom, and freedom to exceed as an athlete. What I understand now is that I still desperately wanted him to be a part of my development, my success, and most importantly my life. I went to great measures in trying to get my father's attention, some of which involved "acting out." I would create this agitation by not responding to or disrespecting my mother's instructions. I knew that if I didn't obey her, she would tell him. My desire for his attention – any attention – was so great that despite the discipline that I knew I was in store for, my fear of punishment wasn't enough to rival the level of satisfaction I got from making him notice me.

All children want to be recognized. As a part of my father's disengagement from the emotional aspects of himself, I wanted to find a way to focus his attention on me and illicit some kind of response from him. Even if it was negative attention, I still wanted it. When boys act out and the father isn't present, a part of the child's mind may know and understand that there's another energy that should be present in the household to help create order. There's a whole dynamic in the relationship between father and son that a child will continue to seek out, even if the father isn't present in the household.

When a man without a father becomes an adult, he must find a constructive way to deal with those unmet emotional needs, including the need to be seen and acknowledged. If he doesn't, that pain and anger and frustration can still erupt periodically as unwanted or negative behavior. For example, a married man may have an affair and end up divorced. An employee may behave badly and, as a consequence, lose a much needed job. A man may abandon his own children, after claiming that he would "never" treat his children the way his father treated him.

It's all acting out of unresolved issues.

Unlike very young children, as adults we come to the understanding that all attention isn't good attention. We want to generate positive, life affirming attention. We want to do what's best for ourselves and for our families, rather than allowing old, unconscious scripts to dictate our behavior or cause rifts between ourselves and those we love.

There are certain things that help us to resolve the urge to act out. Look at the mental chatter that masquerades as your day-to-day thoughts. Take a step back and look at what you're telling yourself. Actively seek out the space to be silent and quiet the mind. Maintain a healthy eating lifestyle. Most people don't think about this aspect, but the truth is that some foods serve as emotional triggers. Healthy eating relates directly to a healthy emotional and behavioral outlook. For example, if you binge eat a bunch of sweets and go on a sugar high, the next time you find yourself craving more sugar you begin to associate the sugar high with relief from the emotional tension that you were feeling. We must understand how to handle our triggers without resorting to unconscious behaviors. Likewise, we need to recognize that there's an extremely strong correlation between one's mental, emotional, spiritual and physical health. We can't neglect one aspect while expecting the others to remain healthy.

It took me many years to begin to understand the ways in which I was still acting out from my hurt, "little boy" self, reacting to the triggers that I experienced as I continued to relive the past. My mind never had a shortage of stories to tell about all the things my father didn't do, or all the ways in which he refused to love and support me.

I remembered times when I'd hurry home to show him my

report card because I'd made all A's. He'd take a glance at the card and respond with "yeah." I could never understand if his response was that of approval or not. I later assumed it to be the latter. I tried over and over to reach his standard for my life, but it seemed as if it wasn't working. Like him, I had a knack for hard work and excellence. I even tried the whole rigid attitude that was pervasive with my dad. Those attempts never quite worked for me. I was too outgoing. I liked being involved in groups and on teams. I never had problems with communicating with others. As a matter of fact, I was always looking for a way to express my self; traits that I know were handed down from my mother. Dad's reservation at home was too firm for me.

My angry attitude toward him began to congeal. Being around him started to become uncomfortable. As I graduated to junior high school and the seventh grade my motto was "do it for me and for my self." As I distanced myself from my dad, I began to resent him more. I thought, What's the use in having him around if he has no interest in being a part of my life? I expressed my thoughts with my mother. She wouldn't necessarily condone his behavior, however it seemed as if she eventually would resolve the matter by in responding in his favor.

"He's proud of you in his own way," she'd say.

She'd always accompany those statements with a mention of her unconditional support of my work and efforts. My mother's words and thoughts were great. But I wanted him to be proud of me too. I wanted to hear it come from his lips and not from someone who was trying to speak on his behalf.

By the time I was a junior in high school, football had become my best friend. I had become a celebrated athlete, garnering interest from some of the country's most coveted football programs. During this time, more than ever before, I secretly wished for my father's support and guidance. Several of my closest friends were being courted by highly touted college programs as well. I noticed how proud their fathers were of them. The support, the concern and the pride were evident. They were at every practice and every game.

My older brother begged my dad to come watch me play. And he finally did. We were having Homecoming and playing against a cross-town rival. We won by over three scores and I continued to add to a stellar year as running back. On my way out of the stadium, I saw my brother standing along the fence near the locker room. Once I walked up to greet him, I noticed dad standing there beside him.

"Look who I brought with me," my brother said.

I glanced at my dad.

"Ya'll put a good whooping on 'em, didn't ya," my father cheered.

"Yeah," I quipped.

I was embarrassed at the sight of him. I was so not used to having him around for support that I didn't know how to respond. I realized during the course of the following week that him attending the game had not altered my thoughts at all. Perhaps we had shredded ties that could never be mended. To protect my self and my feelings, I sided with my thoughts. However, in all honesty, I wasn't fine with this. Deep down my heart sill ached for my father and a way to make things right between us. But repair was hard to imagine, and the pain of the process seemed even more excruciating.

By the time I'd graduated college I had incarcerated my dad in my own mind, resenting him for all that he had done and said to make me feel that my life was fruitless and unworthy. I remember him coming to my college graduation. After a short while, he disappeared from sight.

"Where did daddy go?" I asked.

"He's somewhere around here," my mother answered.

I noticed him standing off in the distance alone, staring at the surroundings. He clearly didn't know how to reach me any more than I knew how to reach out to him.

By the time I landed my first job, I had committed him to solitary confinement. I threw away the key to appeal forever. Very seldom did I say anything to him during that time of my life. Soon the very mention of his name caused me to cringe. When I called home to talk to my mother, she would ask in a suggestive tone if I wanted to talk to him.

"Your daddy is sitting right here, would you like to say hello?"

My answer was always "no."

As dry and emphatic as I could possibly muster out, I wanted to make the point that I wanted nothing to do with him. I did not understand him and I didn't think he understood me. Nor did I think he ever wanted to. That was the most painful part of all. Though we both desired to understand each other, that understanding wouldn't come until many years later. As a child and, then a young man, I didn't understand how to put other people's priorities in perspective. I just saw my own.

I justified distancing myself from my father because I believed that it he was the one trying to get farther away from me. It was too painful to hear my father say, "I can't play with you now" or "I can't stay for your baseball game because I promised somebody else that I was going to be with them." In the mind of a child, it's hard to negotiate those things. Like most children, I agonized over thoughts like, "Why can't my dad stay? Does he not believe in me? Doesn't he want to see me play?" And then it just escalated to, "I may be weird to him. I wonder if he doesn't like me?"

We rarely have the courage to open ourselves up to actually communicate these thoughts. I know that I never had the courage to ask my daddy, "Do you like me?" I had already made up in my mind that he didn't. He didn't want to be around me. Choosing to believe those things was the source of my greatest pains.

Most people know where their pain began, even if they have to go page by page to get back to it. But we need to get to the core of what began this journey of pain and emotional discomfort.

Fatherlessness means something different to each individual. When talking about sons growing up without fathers, there are varying degrees of absence. My father was technically in the home for my entire life, but he was rarely, if ever, present for me. Then you have families where the father has never been physically present. So how do you speak to that sadness, that emptiness? There is one common denominator in each of these scenarios: the questions that the child is left trying to decipher on his own, how should I be as a result of the pain that I'm feeling? How should I act? How should I conduct myself?

When a father is present, he can see when something is going awry in his child's life and he can step in to provide some kind of support and guidance. When the father is not present, its like the child must fend for himself. In the majority of cases, the child's mother is present offering the best support that she is capable of, trying to guide him along. But she will always be contending with the absence of the father figure. Many children are left questioning, what was wrong with me? Just like I did. That was the core of my pain: I believed my father didn't want to be around me because he thought that something was wrong with me. I began to live my life from that construct, wanting to be OK in people's eyes so that they would accept me. I did everything that I possibly could for that to happen.

We want to identify, recognize and acknowledge the pain and the misconceptions that may have held us hostage for so long. When you identify something, it shortens the playing field. You begin to focus on the important details. Recognizing has within it a larger context, where we begin to identify underlying factors. We ask ourselves questions like: What was the underlying theme of all of those things that I recognized in my childhood? For me, I recognized a recurring theme in which I insisted to myself that my father did not want to be around me. He thought that something was wrong with me. I wanted to find any possible way to make him love me.

Acknowledgment is another important key. Sometimes we get so numb that we even stop remembering the painful details. Numbness says that everything is all good, when its not. There is a place inside where you remember the events that have occurred. But you've stacked accolades, good words, titles and money on top of it. These shining accomplishments are heaped on top of a menacing, painful volcano that is going to erupt some day.

Years may have passed. We may have money, responsibilities, and maybe even our own children. We tell ourselves, "I don't need his love anymore." But that's not true. Yes, we do. We don't want to acknowledge that. The love that we needed from our fathers when we were five years old is the love that we need now. But we stack all of the externals on top of our need because at some point we said, "He's never going to do it. I give up!"

We may give up in our minds, but our heart never does.

Looking back, I realized that I wanted my father to be somebody else. I wanted his words to land softer. I wanted him to not take so many emotional sharp turns and twists because they left me feeling foggy and disillusioned. But that was just him. So, I came to the agreement with myself that I was going to allow him to be who he was. I also needed to find the courage within myself to forgive him for those things that I thought were absolutely wrong that he said and did to me. Forgiveness allowed me to unclench my fists; the clenched fists also held my heart in them. I had held onto my heart so tightly that I didn't want anybody to have space in my fist with my heart. I didn't want to be hurt anymore. But when I metaphorically released my fists, I released my heart, and I also released my father. I freed me in the process.

As we free ourselves and move on, we must give up the thoughts of how wrong he was or how he hurt us. In my case I had to let go of the idea, he didn't like me. How do you give up those thoughts? Rather than holding on to or judging the emotionally charged thoughts, try to turn your attention to your process of learning to love yourself. That's not an easy task. But it's an absolutely necessary part of moving forward with peace in your mind and freedom in your heart.

On this journey to greater self-love, ask yourself, who am

I? I've got my father dissected. Let's look at me. Let's find the beauty in me. Let's find the self-acceptance in me. Let's find the self worth in me. We can only work on ourselves.

I had to learn to give myself the unconditional love that I'd always wanted to receive from my father. Our story ended well, because we were ultimately able to meet each other with tremendous love, understanding and mutual respect in the years before my father passed away. But what if we had never reconciled? What if my father had never said that he loved me before he died? I would've been OK. Because I said I loved him. That was good enough. But it took many years to get to that point of clarity. I had to get past disappointment and sadness and my hatred for him to get to forgiveness. Beyond forgiveness is where I got to start living the life that I loved. I started loving me.

Chapter 3

LEAVING THE NEST

The Power of Self-Discovery

Growing up, I patterned my life after what other people thought I should be. Those people had only the best intentions toward me, but the end result was that I discontinued my own path of self-discovery. Instead, I tried to persuade people to like me by being who I thought they wanted me to be. This was especially true of my father. I applied myself to all the things that I thought he would admire and celebrate.

We all like to be affirmed and we'll go to great measures to make people think we're cool. The bottom line is that we want to be accepted. Human beings need connection, which is why it feels so painful to be ostracized. It often seems as though it would be easier to acquiesce to the status quo, what society says is normal, even if it means detaching from the truth of who we are. In my mind, I didn't know what was acceptable in my father's eyes, so I tried everything. Unfortunately, I never really succeeded at getting his acceptance.

Young men want to be accepted in their environments. But they risk losing themselves as they dive into the pressure of social conditioning and, sometimes, the illusions of social grandeur (just think of how larger than life some gangs and gang members can appear in the eyes of an impressionable boy). In the long run, they somehow negotiate away their sense of being authentic and constructive.

When we're trying to acquiesce to someone else's vision of who and what we should be, we must live by the rules and conditions that they've created. When we indoctrinate ourselves into what "they" believe is right or wrong, what "they" see as acceptable or unacceptable, sooner or later conflicts will arise. This is inevitable, because we're not all made to have the same constructs, beliefs, desires or standards. Rather than take on someone else's idea of what life should be and how life should be lived, we must negotiate our own standard of living.

Inside our own standard of living is our true essence. Inside of our authenticity is the seed of genius. But when we take on what someone else deems to be the standard, it may go totally against our creative brilliance. For example, when I was growing up, I had friends who believed (and whose parents believed) that it was OK if they made grades of "B−" or "C+" just as long as they got by in school. That was their standard of excellence. But mine was different. I knew that I could make A's. However, one time, because I wanted these other boys to like me and I wanted to fit into their group, I intentionally made a "C" on one of my papers. When I received the paper back form the teacher, I showed it to them. And it didn't change their minds about me at all whatsoever. They still thought I was the nerdy, snobby little teacher's pet that lived next to them.

At that point, I began to ask myself, do I really want to make "C's"? I can continue to do that if I want to be with that group. But then I had the all-knowing, all wise mother, who said, "Let me see your "C.""

I showed her the paper and she said, "I don't want to see anymore "C's" from you because I know that C is not your best."

And I never brought home another "C" because I had that championing voice echoing my mind. But as precious as my mother's words were to me, as a young boy, I was looking for that voice from my father. I wanted to experience him as that kind of authority figure in my life, the person who would always admonish me to do better.

When that energy wasn't forthcoming from him, I began to act out, to push my limits. People are going to step beyond boundaries; it's just part of stretching and growing. We step beyond boundaries to see where we stand, how we measure up and fit in. But there's a difference in the mindset of the rebellious boundary stepper. That psyche says, I'm doing this in spite of something or someone. That was my case. I couldn't find a way to get answers to my questions about life from my father. So I finally decided that I would go to great ends to get the answers out in the world, my way. And not only would I find those answers my way, I would find them in ways that would support my rebellion. The truth was, what I really needed was to be affirmed.

When young men act out from the need to be acknowledged or affirmed, the results can be devastating. They have babies out of wedlock even when they aren't willing or able to take care of them. Some boys will go out and join gangs. Sometimes, to really rattle the nerves of mothers and grandmothers who are the only supporting characters in their world, they'll stay away from home. They won't come back when they're supposed to, knowing that the women who love and care deeply for them are worrying about them all day and all night. They do this to get attention, to lash out at the only people available to them. When the man whose attention they're really trying to get isn't there to check them, they can step beyond as many boundaries as they want, because he can't do anything about it.

He's not there.

This was the case with my father. Though he was physically present, he was inaccessible. His unwillingness or inability to communicate with me, to answer my tough questions about growing up, left a void in my life that nothing else could fill.

Growing up in the South meant having a great deal of respect for words. There were words that only grown ups could use. There were also words and conversations that were tacitly forbidden to mention—even by the elders. And no matter what type of burning desire you may have had to talk about certain things, the taboo around it had been entrenched by generations of suppression.

As a child, this didn't sit well with me. I wanted to know about everything. If I placed my eyes on it, I wanted to know what it was all about. And like most children, there were things that I could sense in the atmosphere as well. My mother would try and answer most of my questions. When she couldn't quite find a healthy answer, she would ask my sister to fill in. However, there was one subject that I learned never to ask or talk about. As natural as I thought it would be to mention, what I had learned in church and at home made me apprehensive in raising the subject at all.

Sex.

Sex was a dirty word, plain and simple. When I was young, I believed that all kids were sexually curious. I liked touching my private areas because I thought, it's a part of me. Why shouldn't I know about that? If I know about my hands and my feet, why can't that be part of my learning too? But I soon found out that if you mentioned sex at home you would either get a beating or a tongue lashing so harsh that you'd wish to have never been born. If you mentioned the word around peers, they would call you names and ostracize you. The first time that I told my grandmother I had a crush on Betty Jo Taylor, she went into a rage.

"You ain't got no business having a crush on somebody! You are too young!"

She punctuated her thought by reminding me that good little boys don't become "mannish" before their years. The term mannish was used to describe a child who was way out of bounds in conduct. As in, "Girl, you gon' have to get a hold on him. He's mannish!" My daddy even told me, "You too mannish. You gon' end up having to pay for something you not ready for."

"What does that mean?" I would ask.

"You'll find out!" he'd snap. "You keep doing what you doing!"

If you became labeled by the term mannish, you'd find yourself at the back of the social line and the subject of everybody's judging eyes.

Being pushed aside because of a stigma wasn't my idea of fun. Once that barnacle latched onto your name, it was hard to get it off. I knew many young men in my neighborhood that had been labeled with undesirable traits, only to spend nearly a lifetime trying to be initiated back into the good graces of others. I wanted to know the answers to my questions, but I didn't want to know that badly. So, I kept it all to my self, believing that one day I'd have an opportunity to explore that part of me that was yearning to be fully expressed.

As I grew, I developed a heightened awareness of sexuality. I was so sensitive that I could just stand where I was and feel the sexual energy pulsing all around me. For example, I could tell, from the age of about twelve or thirteen, when the women around me were not getting what they needed at home. I knew when their husbands were neglecting them. I could smell it.

When I was fifteen and working as a sack boy at Kroger's Supermarket, I had an affair with a married woman who was more than ten years older than me.

And my mother found out.

The woman's name was Belinda and she was a friend of my mother's who I worked with at Kroger's. She had started calling me when her husband was working out of town, driving his truck. One day, my mother asked me why Belinda was calling me at home. I made up a lame excuse about Belinda needing to give me my work schedule for the week because I was her bagger. My mother was no fool.

She asked me, "So why does Belinda call to give you your schedule every other day? Is she your boss?"

I said, "No, but she has the schedule."

My mother replied, "She should not be calling you to give you your schedule. You should be getting your schedule at the end of the week."

Shortly after this conversation, my mother showed up at

Kroger's, right to Belinda's line where I was bagging groceries.

She looked at me, and she looked at Belinda, and she said, "Hi. How you doing, girl? How do you like your little bagger back there?"

Belinda said, "Oh, he's just fine."

My mother replied, "Um-hm." Then she turned around and walked away.

When I got home that night, the first thing my mother said to me was, "You leave her alone. She's married. And her husband, if he comes home and catches you or even thinks that you've been playing around with her, he'll hurt you. You stay away from her. Do you understand me? Have you been over to her house?"

"No, not yet."

"You better not let me catch you over there. Has she been up here?"

"Yes," I said sheepishly. "She brought me home from work."

"What did you do?"

"Nothing."

I didn't tell my mother that Belinda actually used to wait for me if she had a shift that ended before mine. Truthfully, I was glad my mother told me to stay away from her. That situation had just been another way for me to rebel, because I wanted to fit in somewhere. I wanted someone to think that I was cool.

That's what I thought I wanted. What I really wanted was for my father to sit me down and say, "Son, don't sacrifice a brilliant career that you have ahead of you for that. The woman that you choose, whatever you choose, will be ten times more beautiful than her."

I wanted him to talk to me, man to man, about relationships

and women and falling in love and growing into manhood.

But he didn't.

When I was old enough to date openly and establish relationships, I was careful not to talk too much about it with anyone. My father, of course, warned me of protecting my self and my friend from pregnancy by using condoms.

"Don't bring no babies in hear unless you are gonna take care of 'em," he cautioned.

He was the only one in my family that gave me a glimpse of how to navigate the meandering mind and physical urges of a teenage boy. Although we never talked about it again, his tone was enough to inform my entire being. I made it through my adolescent years unscathed.

As an adult, I can understand now what my parents were trying to communicate. Back in the day, having babies out of wedlock was a jail sentence, a welcome to a life of struggle. For my parents, part of their survival dictated keeping a leash on their physical desires, lest they end up paying a price that was too steep and that they simply couldn't afford.

But when young people rebel, part of that acting out behavior stems from the fact that they'll do just about anything to get attention from the adults in their lives. For me, the great divide was sex. I wanted to know more about how I got here. That seemed like it should have been a healthy, friendly conversation. But with my father, the most I could get out of him was, "You ain't supposed to be asking those kinds of questions."

Why wouldn't I have asked my father? His reaction didn't make sense to me. He just wasn't available. It could've been that he was afraid to ask his father those same kinds of questions because he felt like his father would have said the same things to him. Or maybe he did ask his father those questions and received the same answer he gave me. Either way, his responses did nothing to satisfy my need to know.

I became more curious about my sexuality and just how far I could stretch my imagination. The energy I had as a teenager followed into my years of developing into a young man. For a while, though, I was able to successfully channel those repressed energies into other pursuits, namely a chance at higher education.

I decided that it was time to leave the nest for good. College was calling, along with the possibility of achieving the dream I'd held for years—to play professional football. I tried with all of my might and strength to land a spot on a professional roster, but it never happened. My hopes of playing football on Sundays never materialized and I wondered what else could give me the satisfaction and purpose that I honestly believed living the life of a celebrated athlete would offer. I finally came to accept that playing professional football wasn't meant for me.

I had garnered the interest of two Fortune 500 companies by the end of my senior year of college. I was offered the position of Marketing Representative by both firms. Though I didn't take the offers lightly, anything other than a Sunday stroll up and down the field fell short in my mind. International Paper, my first offer was an outstanding company with a strong reputation as being tops in its category. IBM, who later offered me a position, had an edge. Not just an edge on International Paper, but an edge on every other company on the list.

As my mother put it, "You made it to the top, son; a great salary, opportunity for unlimited growth, tenure…and all those benefits!"

IBM was at the top of the corporate heap; number one on the Fortune 500 Hundred list. Without hesitation, I accepted their offer. Excited that I had made what I thought was a good choice, I decided to share with dad. My hope was that he too would be thrilled for me.

"Big Blue," he commented. "Where do they have you working?"

I named all of the states and territories of coverage: West Memphis, North Central Mississippi, Eastern Arkansas, and the Boot Hill of Missouri.

"You be careful out there," was all he said.

A short, yet hopeful conversation, I thought. This may be a ground we can start planting and building relationship. Still, there was something missing. In my mind I had hoped that he would jump out of his seat with joy at my announcement.

"Congratulations, son! I'm so proud of you, man," were the words that I was wishing for. Landing a job like this would surely warrant a celebration. But all I got was "be careful" and "watch where you're going."

On my ride back home I contemplated that five-minute talk the entire way. For three hours I tried dissecting his words to make them somehow change to what I desired for him to say. But that was a futile hope where my father was concerned. Why did I think this time would be different? This was the way that he'd always responded to me. I'd still hoped that he'd be proud enough of me to show a little affection.

Ironically I passed a billboard that stated: Jesus Cares for YOU. As the Christian boy that I had become, in that moment that sign only added fuel to my bitter disappointment. I didn't give a damn if Jesus cared. I wanted my daddy to care. That's all I wanted.

Unfortunately (for my mother, not for me) my corporate career didn't last very long. Within a few short years, I'd decided to give up marketing and move to New York to pursue a newly found desire to be a professional performer. It was one of the most exciting times of my life. Although I'd never lived outside of southern borders, New York offered an opportunity for me to stretch as a performing artist as well an individual.

I remember wanting to share the news of my leaving for the Big Apple with my father; however the thought of talking with him about it made me nervous. For some reason I believed that he would disapprove, and that he would reprimand my choice to relocate by verbally pointing out why he thought I wasn't ready to make such a move. I did however rush it past his ears, just to see what he'd say.

"New York is a big place," he said. "You be careful up there, and remember to watch your back at all times."

Good advice, I thought. At least he hadn't insisted that I go to see a psychiatrist, like my mother had proposed.

New York, to say the least, didn't carry with it the friendly, tactful fiber of the South. It was tough, rugged, and sometimes downright nasty. What you saw was what you got, and even some of what you didn't see would sneak up on you in a blinking second. Somewhere along the way, in my southern upbringing, I had developed an ability to focus while in stream with the seeming chaos. New York offered a universal buffet of things, conditions, and personalities, always careening from one end of the spectrum to the other. This was far from the small community that I grew up in where everybody knew your name as well as your parents and grandparents. A small group of settlers had established our town that had grown into a tight knit community. It was an extended family of sorts, where casual conversation and manners were the norm and where we were lulled to sleep on a summer's night by the sound of crickets in high grass. This was not a bad way to spend life. It just wasn't how I wanted to spend the rest of mine.

In New York, I could escape all of what the South represented for me: a traditional march to the beat of old drums, as well as the hovering clouds of my relationship with my father. The latter was the underlying reason that made the move so appealing to me. Being away from him seemed like the best thing I could've ever done at the time.

New York City had a charm of its own. If it wasn't someone bumping into you with full force on the sidewalk, it was braving winter's relentless cold and struggling to keep your stride on some of the busiest sidewalks in the world. The summers had days of blistering heat. There were pockets in the city where the stench from a trashcan's overflow would attack your senses as you passed by, even causing severe nausea. I refused to let any of it deter me from my dream of performing on the Broadway stage.

But while this new life of being a performing artist was beginning to show some promise, there remained a void. I couldn't quite explain it, other than the need to be noticed and loved. That old energy was being stirred back to life inside me, with no one around to try to squelch or repress it. In fact, the city seemed to be welcoming me with open arms.

New York is a world bazaar. Everything is seemingly available. From the moment you walk out of the door your senses are pushed into overload–people packed streets, yellow cabs whizzing down the avenue, animals bustling past, and billboards hawking consumer items from A to infinity. There was also the scent of those things hidden from the naked eye. It doesn't take a rocket scientist to figure out that underneath the visual circus of Manhattan is the world bursting with other types of habits and ways to fulfill them.

In New York, I decided that I wanted to know much more about what my parents and community had tried to hide from me for so many years. I was a grown man, and I wanted to experience what sex was all about without a whole bunch of warnings or expectations placed on my behavior. And because of the nature of that city, where sex is everywhere, I got it wherever I went. I could smell it wafting in the air of a friendly breeze like a raccoon sniffing out his next meal.

I wasn't aware of it at the time, but I was still acting out the same old rebellious pathologies. In my mind I thought, Hmmm, I know this drill. I know it so well. And I'm going to play it out.

Sex was as fluid as the streets in the Big Apple. Every avenue you crossed was an opportunity in finding someone to engage. I had found a particular love for the feel of being with somebody new. The social seduction, the short conversation, and the act were all intoxicating to me. The more sex I had the more I wanted. Sex was my drug of choice. I put my childish charm into full motion. Subconsciously I was fulfilling my desire to seek and conquer. This was my way of getting what I thought I wanted, and to some extent, what I thought I needed. I never used drugs or alcohol as a stimulant or while I was having sex, but the effect of my amplified sexual behavior was enough to send me into a social oblivion. Sometimes my only purpose of taking someone back to my apartment was my selfish pursuit of gaining more ground on what had obviously become my obsession. It happened so often that I became completely desensitized to my authentic self.

This unconscious state of behavior continued for months. However, I began noticing that the "fun" of it had begun to tarnish. Sometimes my desire would start dying away before we could get our clothes off. The impulse to kick them out of my bed once we were finished was only calmed by feeling that I had somehow violated their integrity. Then I had an encounter that would change the course of my sexual behavior and my life.

One day, I had sex with three different people, one after another. I went back to my apartment in Harlem and I sat on the edge of my bed. At that moment, I had a spiritual experience where I saw myself in spirit form sitting over in the corner. Then my perspective transferred over to where my spirit man was looking at my shell, my body. He was dejected, exhausted and dazed.

I took a long nap. When I woke up, I said, "God, I can't do this anymore. I don't want to do this anymore."

From that instant forward, I began to discover that there was something else that I was really after. I was a grown man, living on my own far away from home, but I was still acting out because somewhere in my soul I was still searching for the love that I wanted to experience from my father. What would that love give me? I asked myself. The answer came back: It would give me self worth. It would give me self-esteem. And it would give me power.

No amount of sex, money, or notoriety could provide those things. I was a grown man, and yet I was still waiting for my father to give me his approval, to tell me that I was all right. And because that hadn't happened, I went out searching for that validation everywhere else. When I looked at that shell sitting on my bed, he was absolutely powerless. He had negotiated every part of his being, everything that he had known about integrity, health, dignity, and compassion. It was all out the door for a quick fix.

Any kind of rebellious behavior—be it sex, drugs, gangs or any overly obsessive behavior—prevents us from experiencing the true satisfaction that we're seeking. The satiation that masquerades as satisfaction is usually only present in the very beginning. True satisfaction is when you understand that what you're doing is not only benefitting you, but it's also benefitting whomever you're involved with. That's a healthy relationship.

We're not always taught healthy habits and healthy ways of being. In many cases we are not taught that healthy relationships are about giving your best to someone and allowing them to give their best to you so that you can both prosper. Healthy relationships aren't about giving something with the expectation of receiving something else in return. And then, when the person doesn't give us what we want, we get mad. We feel cheated that we didn't get what we thought we needed.

There is a tremendous difference between healthy self-discovery and rebellion. I had become a connoisseur of sex. I got to a place where I was having as much sex as I possibly could because I thought that's what I wanted. But my actions really stemmed from a need inside of me to have someone say, "You're OK." Sex became a drug and a way for me to convince myself that I was desirable. But then it turned sour. I was trying to get something from it that had nothing to do with the act itself. I thought I would get the answers to those questions of acceptance. But the fulfillment that I was seeking continued to elude me. Sex became pointless after awhile.

On the surface, I had everything I'd ever wanted. I toured internationally with some of the best stage shows in the world and finally made my dream of singing on a Broadway stage into a reality. In a profession known to be fickle and demanding, I worked continuously. Jesus Christ Superstar…Smokey Joe's Café… Europe… The Lion King on Broadway… I was like a child in a candy store, believing that I had discovered this whole world of cookies and candy. But there was something inside of me that was never fully satisfied.

Sooner rather than later, all of those candy stores became depleted. The feelings of inadequacy that I thought I was wiping away never really went anywhere. They were just suppressed for a while, waiting for the right time to resurface. And when they hit, they hit hard because my mind could no longer contain all of the disappointment. My heart was crying. My heart, which contained that spiritual umbilical cord of communication and love that I had for my father was now speaking to me.

As young men, we can leave the nest mentally and emotionally well before we grow old enough to leave the nest physically, and venture out into the world on our own. When I arrived in New

York for the first time to pursue my acting career, one of the predominant thoughts running through my mind was, "I'm out of the south… and I'm far away from him." I thought I was discovering things about myself that I needed to experience. What I really discovered was that I could never, ever get far enough away from the love I had for my father to truly escape it. Leaving the nest, in the end, gave me a platform for return.

I left my home physically but could not escape mentally. I don't regret my experiences in New York and I strongly believe that, at times, we do need to take a physical retreat. Whether it's for five years or five months or five days, a physical retreat provides our eyes with another picture to look at. But what we can't really get away from is the innate need to be loved and to love. When we realize that those cords are much deeper than any physical distance, then we open ourselves to the powerful call of authentic self-discovery and the rediscovery of those whom we love.

When I moved to New York, I believed I wanted to get away from my father and never be around him again. That's what my head said. My heart said, it's too painful to be around him, because I love him so much that being physically away from him will give me a moment of peace and rest as I navigate my way through the world and try to figure things out.

As we grow, there are different levels of what we consider self-acceptance and self-worth and power and self-esteem. We can get from powerless to powerful by engaging ourselves in conversation to uncover our true desires and motivations. We become powerful by engaging in relationships that will sharpen those parts of ourselves. At the basic level, we go back to asking the question, where am I still trying to be accepted. Where am I still lacking self-esteem and self-worth? Where did that stem from? Recognizing the genesis of those beliefs can give us an indication of where we're still trapped in a cycle of repetitive pain.

We must begin to expose those places where we feel inadequate, or that we're not worth investing the time to become more active in our pathway towards wholeness. It's imperative to make the time to be with our self, and to be around things and people that exude self-worth and purpose. One of the simplest ways to do this is to get out into nature. Go for a walk. Sit down in the middle of a garden. Be with those things that have no ulterior motive. They aren't trying to outdo or outrun anything. They are stationary in their purpose and they are fine with what they are. There are many things we could learn from taking a few minutes to meditate on our relationship with nature.

Begin to create a dialog with people who have healthy conversations. Sometimes people in your life may have to fall away from you, including longtime friends or even family members. But we have to understand what is important to us and begin to live our lives according to that standard. If our children are important to us, then we can understand that the way that we conduct our lives and the things that we say are going to have an affect on the way that they live.

We must learn to be versatile in the ways that we think of ourselves. There's a decoding that has to happen. In the decoding, we learn to become compassionate with ourselves, releasing self-condemnation. Contrary to what we may think, self-condemnation ads fuel to the fire of rebellion, blame and unhappiness. We don't reign in our behavior; we spiral more out of control. True freedom provides a conscious awareness of being all of who you are in the context of optimum health and wellbeing, where we're not destroying ourselves to make a point. We're not eating away our lives or drugging away our lives, trying to find peace. That's not peace.

We all want to feel that we're alive, that we're loved and wanted. We try to mimic those feelings by many other means that can only end in death, whether it be the death of our purpose, our self-esteem, our creative excellence and sometimes even our bodies. When we're able to separate our authentic selves from our perceived lack (left over from the pain of neglect and abandonment) we enter the path of honest self-actualization and discovery. This is real freedom, which is completely different from having the license to do what we want to do, when we wan to do it.

From this space of freedom, we receive the spiritual permission to live the very best life that we can. That permission activates qualities that may have been dormant thus far in your life. Joy is one. When we sit at the table of joy, we invite ourselves to a world of possibilities. Joy is a sibling of creative genius. Creative genius is an ambassador to the world, whatever world you want to create for yourself.

When we act out or rebel or overindulge in unhealthy behaviors, we're using our power of creation in self-destructive ways. We can break that cycle and channel the energy of creation into powerfully self-affirming ways of being. Taking small, every day actions toward self-actualization and fulfillment gives courage the permission to continue to walk with you as you grow and move forward.

I still walk this path daily. My old thoughts that my father had abandoned me didn't magically disappear as I began to heal. But when they came, I was able to say to myself, yes, that might have been true, but now I have a new understanding of what's real to me and what life means to me. The thoughts will come. As a matter of fact, they never go away. Not permanently. But when the painful or unhealthy thoughts come into my awareness, rather than acting them out, I recognize them for what they are to me. A call to prayer.

Feeling abandoned by my father led me to have an intense need for affirmation in other areas of my life. As my drug of choice, I realize that my sex drive controlled me. Now I can recognize those urges for what they are, creative energy. I can call upon my creative genius and can do something with that energy. That gives me the opportunity to choose the fulfillment of love over the drive for sex.

We want to take our impulse toward creativity and self-discovery and channel it into life affirming pursuits. When we're engaging in healthy behavior, its not just healthy for us, it's healthy for everyone. It creates an environment of harmonious living. It gives us an indication of how we can be brilliant within ourselves, and contagious to the world around us.

Chapter 4

THE JOURNEY BACK IN

The Power of Compassion

C ompassion is a powerful component of self-love, which is essential for us to understand on a deeper level as we move forward on this journey toward healing and self-discovery. It is integral to our ability to release toxic emotional habits like shaming and blaming and criticizing. Compassion makes it so that we can all come out on the winning side. No one is incarcerated. We free the captives so to speak, and in doing so we free ourselves. When we embrace compassion, we allow ourselves to give oxygen to the places that have been constricted in our minds for such a long time, so that a new breath of fresh air can provide a new possibility for how our issues can be resolved.

On the other hand, when we deny our compassion, choosing instead to blame others for our experiences, we cut off our ability to transcend our circumstances. Blame is where we've chosen to believe something about what someone else did to us, or what we did to ourselves, to the extent that we're no longer willing to look at how our consciousness can be shifted. Blame is a victim's tool. When we want to a scapegoat for what we think is wrong with us, we blame someone else for the way that we turned out.

Compassion gives us a chance to give our brains a rest, metaphorically speaking. Visualize this with me: see the relaxation, the expansiveness of our thoughts actually increasing the blood flow to the brain so we can think differently. We're now able to oxygenate those places where we've cut off any semblance of life. New pathways in our brains begin to flourish, providing fresh mental and emotional connections that allow us to perceive life differently and begin to make different choices.

When we can see the events of our lives differently, from an expanded vantage point, we become willing to believe in a brand new possibility for our relationships and circumstances. Compassion often comes as a result of us having some kind of fallout with someone. At least, that's where the opportunity to practice compassion is born, because that's normally where the blame begins—even if the person that we're blaming is ourselves.

I know more than my fair share about blame. I blamed my father for so many years for causing me such pain all through my life. Even after making the conscious choice to forgive him many years ago, I still found myself reliving old slights in my mind from time to time. And, sure enough, the feelings of blame and judgment would be right there waiting. But I received a life-changing opportunity to release blame and practice compassion in September of 2009.

I'd decided to spend a few months with my parents in Nashville. As it turned out, I became a student of compassion while I was there. Of course, I was unaware of what was about to occur when I first decided to go home. I didn't know that I had come back to sit in the classroom again. I thought to myself, I can do my work from Nashville for about six months while helping them. But I didn't know that I had gone back for my own lesson.

I loaded up my SUV and drove cross-country from Los Angeles. I hadn't made a trek that long since my initial tour from Nashville to the west coast five years earlier. I was in full swing in my work of singing at churches and spiritual centers around the country. Months earlier, I'd scheduled myself to be guest vocalist at local centers and speaker on college campuses in the southeastern states, just so I could be with family.

This would be a unique time, since I hadn't spent more than ten consecutive days at home with my parents since my junior year of college. Once I'd graduated and began working, time spent with mom and dad was limited. I called home every day, but I never found the need or time to visit as much.

But that year, my father had been diagnosed with end stage renal disease and had begun his treatments. He went to dialysis every Monday, Wednesday and Friday. I knew that his treatments had been rough on him, but I had no idea how rough until I saw him again. In fact, it took me about a month and a half to come to terms with what had transpired in both of my parents' lives the time between me leaving as a teenager and returning home for an extended period as a grown man.

My parents had slowed down drastically. My father was showing a rapid decline in his health due to the dialysis and a host of other circumstances. He was taking a slew of medicines just to help him maintain his conditions. None of those medications had been able to help him get better. When I first saw my father, I watched him in disbelief. I couldn't believe that he was so thin and frail. He'd always been slim, but fit and extremely active.

Now his skin was sallow. He'd been robbed of all his energy to the point where even walking was a strain. For my part, I walked around in quiet disbelief trying to make sense of all the changes that we were facing.

After being disturbed by his physical condition, I became very selfish and angry. I wanted my father to be the man that I knew growing up. That man was always going, always moving about. Beneath my childish thoughts was the very real fearing of his impending death. I'd never been without him. And even though the years of bad blood between us may have been hard, for him to not be there was an even heavier weight to bear. My father and I had just begun to try to get back to some semblance of what a healthy father/son relationship could look like. The thought of losing him at this point broke my heart.

From there, I went through deep sadness. I cried after watching him shuffle down the ten or twenty yards back to his room after being on dialysis and I felt so sad for him. All of the emotions began to mount. That was my daddy that these things were happening to. My dad had always been an adventurer and a proponent of freedom. Regardless of what I may have said, I had modeled myself after my father. I, too, was an adventurer. Seeing my father from this new perspective gave me the desire to make things better for him. The fast collapse of his health had not just stolen years from his life, but his freedom as well.

There really wasn't much I could do for him. But it made me look at my own mortality because I was half his age. To see him, the adventurer that he was, being limited to sitting on his porch lest the sun or the elements drain his body of what strength he had left, spoke to me about my own being. I realized that I always want to be a proponent and a student of freedom. And freedom can mean a lot of things. As I continued to do my own work, my course in freedom began to change.

I'd always considered myself free because I lived my life as I pleased. For the first time, I found myself wondering where had the time gone. Those early years as an IBMer learning the corporate game, and then my years in New York City pursuing a career as a performing artist seemed to have breezed by. How fast could those eight years living in The Big Apple have passed? Then, a bold but divine trek across the country and five years in Los Angeles. The twenty plus years that had passed set my parents well past the age of retirement by the time I returned home to visit.

Yes, I spent many of those early days feeling sad and helpless. Sometimes memories from the past would surface in my mind and I'd find myself feeling angry, too. Even after everything that had transpired, that anger could still grab hold of me. But I couldn't hang on to the angry thoughts. The anger would come, as I thought about situations that had occurred when I was younger. But the feeling would dissipate quickly because I realized that my father had changed. The change on his part had begun to soften me. In the end, I realized that this was no longer about my feelings about him. It was about helping him live his best life for the remainder of the time he had on earth.

Watching my parents grow older had never been high on my to-do-list. My image of them as vibrant and youthful stayed lodged in my mind. My parents were active people all their lives. When I was growing up, both of them worked long hours during the week. Mom would come directly from work and begin cooking and preparing dinner. Very seldom did we eat out at restaurants – as a matter of fact, I cannot remember ever eating out with my parents.

On Saturdays, after a long week of physically demanding work, we'd get up early to clean the house. We cleaned and dusted the house from end to end. I would get up early so that I could get plenty of Bugs Bunny cartoons and Soul Train before starting. It would usually be me, my mother, and my sister left to clean up. My brother would often find a way to get out having to participate, and daddy would exempt himself.

After our cleaning ritual was complete, we'd spend the day with my mother and her immediate family. Mom came from a cohesive family, eight children in all. We would all congregate at my grandmother's house on Saturday to eat fish and spaghetti. My house was a rock's throw from my mother's birthplace, and most times, mom and I would make the trip on foot. The aroma of delicious food would fill the air as soon as we crossed busy Nolensville Road. Mom would insist on holding my hand until we made it safely across the street, then she'd turn my hand loose and let me sprint off to catch up to all the happenings.

All my aunts, uncles, and cousins would course through my grandmother's tiny three-room house getting our fill of family, fellowship, and plenty of food. These weekends were on going. The only thing that could disrupt our weekly get-togethers would be inclement weather. But even sleet or snow could hardly stop the Saturday ritual, since most of the families lived in close proximity of my grandmother's house just like we did.

Dad would come home on Friday after work, eat a hearty dinner and make it to bed as early as he could because Saturdays for him were his play day with friends. I remember him getting up as early as five o'clock in the morning during the winter months to go squirrel and deer hunting with his friends. He'd be gone the entire day. In the evening, he'd stagger in spent, smelling of a long day's course of cigarettes and beer, and with his day's prize in his hand.

"Look what I got you," he'd say to me. "Take these in there and let your momma skin 'em so we can have them for dinner tomorrow."

I did not like eating anything with a long, bushy tail. I had tasted squirrel meat once before, and I knew that I didn't have the taste for it. But, according to dad, it made for some good eating.

Though he never went to extremes, dad could make his way through a case of beer in a short period of time. And I must admit, the look and smell of those freshly brewed hops in that tall, clear glass made me curious as to how it tasted. Every now and then, when no one was looking or when dad had left an unattended glass on the table, I would take a big swig to quench my curiosity. I would run to my room to swallow it, savoring every moment of that big gulp of Pabst "Blue Ribbon" beer in my mouth.

Sundays were anything but a day of rest at my house. Both my parents would rise early to start their day of activity. If not at church, mom would meet the doors as they opened at the nearest super market. Usually her Sunday meal was prepared on Saturday evening. Sunday's were for any forgotten items needed to add to Sunday's meal or a quick start on the following week's menu. Dad would find a place to socialize with his friends while watching football.

Even until the time that I left home for college, my parents were rarely caught in slow motion. They seemed to be always on a mission and en route to somewhere important. By the time I had returned home for my extended stay, all those years of high gear movement pace had passed.

Witnessing the change in my parents sent me through every emotion imaginable: sadness, fear, frustration, anger and denial. It was only after I'd exhausted myself running in emotional circles, that I began to experience the first stirrings of acceptance and then compassion. When that occurred, my entire outlook changed. I began to see the blessing that was hidden inside this very difficult circumstance. I began to view both my parents, and my self through the eyes of unconditional love and non-judgment.

Compassion is a spiritual quality that holds within it a vortex of energy. The most powerful point of compassion is the self. When we are able to have compassion for our own missteps and shortcomings, we're able to be more loving and generous toward others. When people are willing to look through your mistakes and missteps (because most of us know when we've taken a misstep or when we've crossed the lines of disrespect) when compassion is shown to us in those moments, it does something to the mind and heart. It allows us to release the angst around what we know that we've done. Through that release, it becomes possible to engage a whole new point of view and a whole new way of being without the baggage of shame or guilt. In that instant, we are able to say, "I want to do better. I want to be better."

Now, the question becomes, are there tools in place for us to step into that new way of thinking and being? That's what compassion does: it changes the conversation that we're having with ourselves and the conversations that we have with others. It allows us to release the past and move forward free of old baggage and beliefs. When grudges are held, we feel it, because we're energetic beings. If I have a problem with you and we meet, you can tell that the anger is still there. You can sense my feelings. But if I come up to you, after I've released the feelings from inside of me, and I say, "You know what? I want us to be friends again." And then, when I hug you, you can feel that too.

Somebody has to take the initial step towards compassion. It's normally that way with these universal principles. When you cultivate the courage to move toward compassion, you may find yourself saying something like, "I want to fight for my relationship with my father. I don't care what his actions were in the past. I now choose to see him for who he is and I see the best of him and I want to let him know that."

Before that change occurred in my life, I would've said it was impossible. It would never happen. But it did. Surrendering to compassion helped provide a space for a new energy and a new dialogue to unfold in our relationship. One day, I went into my father's room, I spoke to him like I'd never spoken to him before.

I said, "Daddy, how you doing? Is there anything that I can get you?"

Like I said before, I knew that my father was a king when I was a child coming up. As an adult, I made the transition and came back to that place of honoring him yet again. All of those years where I felt like I had thrown his crown to the ground and stomped on it until all the jewels had fallen off were allowed to fade into the background of my awareness.

Finally, I was able to pick that crown up and say, "Hey, man, I see you. And I want to do anything I can for you. Not because I feel sorry for you. It's because I love you."

If there's any time to make it right, it's right now. Compassion says, I will look beyond what I've thought about you for years and see the true essence of your heart. I will act accordingly because I also have compassion for my self. It's hard to have compassion for someone else if you're beating yourself into the ground. If someone beats himself or herself into the ground and then tries to claim that they have compassion for others, I'm here to say that that's not compassion.

That type of behavior can be a form of annihilation of the self. In beating yourself up and then trying to appease someone else, you're trying to get something from them that you think you don't already have. Compassion has nothing to do with getting something from somebody else. It is all about giving and knowing that, in your giving, reciprocity is happening at that same time; you're giving and receiving. But there's nothing tangible that you need from that other person.

Part of having compassion for ourselves is coming into the awareness that you don't need anything from anyone to validate who you are. We are already perfect, whole and complete as spiritual beings. But sometimes that truth can be hard to see. Not having a loving, healthy father figure in our lives affects self-worth, self-esteem and our ability to discover who we really are. This can make it difficult to have compassion for ourselves when, somewhere deep in our hearts or our subconscious minds, we've long considered ourselves to be lacking or not good enough.

Self-discovery is much easier to talk about than it is to engage in. The process brings up a lot of questions that many of us are tentative in asking. Somewhere deep inside we know that, at some point, we're going to have to face these questions. But, we don't know if we have the tools to face the challenges that these questions pose because we haven't really been taught what self-discovery looks like. Think about it. How many times in school did you even hear the word self-discovery?

How many times in school were you encouraged to meditate or to be silent? Turn your cell phones off for a minute, this generation. Stop tweeting. Stop texting. And for those of us who are well into our adulthood: stop listening to family and trying to get validation from someone else who doesn't have responsibility over your life anymore. Generation after generation, we've been taught the social codes embedded in our traditional verbal communication. Mama knows best. Don't leave the nest. Stay close to home. Sometimes we have to do away with what we think we know in order to get to the truth of who we really are.

In looking at ourselves from a whole different perspective, we have to continue to question all of our basic assumptions. Ask yourself: Who am I and what do I think about me? Regardless of the good, the bad, the indifferent and the awful stuff that people have said about me, what do I think about me? Now, is the time to look in the mirror and do some self-counseling. Most people don't want to look at themselves. They will search to find the newest outfit, the hottest computer generated gadget, the latest piece of technology, the most delicious chocolate cake recipe, or the newest drug, to alter their focus. They believe that by taking the focus off of themselves and placing it on something else, it will give them some kind of indication of who they are. But that's not how it works. Growth and discovery are an inside journey.

Most of the time, people don't tell us that we already have the answers inside. We have our own ability to look at what we are and what we've done and ask the hard questions, and then to be silent enough to hear the honest answers that arise in our awareness. But it takes a concerted effort to find out the truth of who we really are. Once we dive into those questions, we'll begin to understand the importance of what those answers entail in terms of how we move forward in our lives.

Who am I? What did I come down here for? What's important to me?

Ask these kinds of questions and then look at how you're serving those desires and intentions now. If you're already active in the ways that you want to continue to serve those intentions, then so be it. But if you're ready for a change, then you're about to step fully into the realm of self-discovery. After all, the only thing that we really have down here is our being.

Numbing the Pain

I remember my first day of baseball practice. Dad drove me there. Like any normal five year old, I was eager to meet my teammates and get started. As we pulled into the parking lot, I could see all the parents with their sons on the field chatting amongst themselves. Dad put the car in park. I was about to hop out of the car when I turned to him and asked if he was coming.

Of course he wouldn't miss the first day of my baseball career, I thought.

"No. I have some other things to do. I'll be back in about an hour to pick you up", he said.

My disappointment was sharp, but short lived, fading into a realm of excitement that I had never experienced before. As the season progressed, I became a better and better ball player. I was the most versatile player on the team, and the fastest, often rotating between shortstop, second base, and center field. I was just as reliable handling a bat. Coach batted me fourth in the line up. For most of the players, this was our first year at organized baseball - all first graders, all beginners, and most important, all proud to be members of the Tusculum Hardware baseball team.

While in the dugout preparing to bat, I would search the stands to see if dad was around. I wanted desperately for him to see me play – to see me throw the ball and hit the ball. The rumor in the community that we grew up in was that my dad could hit a ball past the tallest tree in the neighborhood. I wanted to be the great baseball player that he was claimed to be.

Seasons passed. Baseball was my pride and joy for the first six years of schooling. I made the All-Star team nearly every year, garnering awards along the way. However, my greatest award would have been having my father attend one of my games. But he never did. The pain mounted. Though I never discussed it with him, I began to resent him. By the time I'd graduated grammar school, I'd stopped expecting anything from him. I guess in a way it was better for me because I had become numb to the pain. He became like an illusion. I could see him but his presence in my life was non-existent.

When we aren't willing to look honestly and deeply at our emotions, the quick fix response is to simply numb those emotions, especially pain and vulnerability. We begin to blame other people for how we feel. So, if you're feeling a certain way and you don't want to continue to have that experience, you immediately begin to blame the person, situation or circumstance where you believe the feeling initiated. Some people, in order to avoid dealing with the source of their unhappiness or figuring out why they've numbed their emotions, will go out and begin to expand their habits.

There are many habits that we use as coping mechanisms to help us avoid dealing with our pain. For some people it's eating. For some people it's over consuming goods. For some people it's drugs. For some people it's sex. For some people it's isolation from the world. Whether you start out engaging in these behaviors consciously or unconsciously, in the end most people become unconscious to them because in the habit of repeating a behavior, you become numb to the fact that you're doing it to excess. You may even forget the reason you started doing it in the first place. After a while, the habit feels like it's serving you because it's pleasurable in the short term. But it never fills the void within.

Sometimes, in order to get out of the old habits and cycles, something has to happen to get your attention that will throw you off the hamster wheel. Perhaps you head so far down the path that you run into a dead end. All of a sudden you wake up and you see that you've taken a course that has led you to nowhere. It surely isn't what you thought it would lead you to. So, you begin to ask the question, "Where am I going with this? Has this habit really satisfied me? Has it filled the void that I thought it would fill?" The answer will always be no.

Running into walls and dead ends in life can actually be a good thing. It helps you to wake up and become conscious if you've been running from something that you didn't want to deal with. Giving yourself license to do whatever you want may feel freeing in the sense that you don't have to be regulated by someone else's thoughts or conditions. But then the behavior may spiral out of control because you think that you have power over something that eventually takes power over you. It disconnects you from your ability to discern whether or not your behavior is healthy for your overall wellbeing.

Allowing yourself to remain numb is the equivalent of running on a hamster wheel. You think you're going somewhere but you're not. After you have exhausted your habit (or after the habit has exhausted you) then you look up and become conscious to where you're really standing in that moment. Chances are that you'll realize that you haven't moved forward. At that particular time you get to ask yourself, am I ready to move forward. If the answer is, No, I still want to find another habit to consume my time and fill the void, then you'll do that. You'll just move over to another wheel that's parallel to the first wheel and jump on the new wheel. Of course, you can still have compassion for yourself even if you make that choice. Healing is a process. There are many steps involved to both healing and compassion. Your first step toward compassion may be simply to say, I'm going to treat myself better by not judging myself so harshly anymore.

When the habits consume us to the point where we feel like we have to have those things to make us all right, then they can eventually turn into a vicious cycle of repetitive procrastination. We think we're moving along, but we're really not. We've just found something to appease the pain that the numbness is masking.

One thing that gets us away from being consumed by our habits is to ask the question, what's really important to me? I think every person has to come to the realization that there's something or someone, other than their own self, that's important to them in the process of becoming aligned with compassion. But if you find yourself unable to change even after coming to the awareness of how certain thoughts, beliefs or habits may be holding you back, please recognize that you are still in a powerful place of growth. You are now conscious. You now have the ability to have a conversation with both the old and new concepts that you wrestle with in your mind.

Anytime we have conversations with ourselves, which I call self-counsels, questions always come up so that we can get to the heart of why we do what we do, or say the things we say. We can look at the ways we act. This gets us to ask the question, where does my behavior come from?

An integral component of self-realization is getting to the point of taking full responsibility for loving ourselves. The journey of self-discovery requires us to realize that we do matter, and that what we do matters in the world. What we say matters. Part of the journey lies in celebrating our goodness, our wise decisions, the parts of ourselves of which we're most proud, in addition to mining the depths. Staying aware of our light helps us to move through this journey without giving in to the voices of self-criticism and judgment that may look to undermine the process.

Taking responsibility for this process moves us away from victimhood. Part of victim consciousness stems from false "realizations" about who we are and how we're lacking and what we never had and what others have done to us in the past. True realization speaks to the fact that we're still here, and that we still have the opportunity of moving forward. We've done some things in the past that were good, in addition to anything that we may have done wrong. Normally, our thought process jumps to the things we feel we need to improve. And we all do have ways to improve. But we also have strengths. Let's begin to talk to our strengths. Healing can happen when we choose to affirm ours self and others, including our fathers.

Somewhere along the line, we're going to have to pull ourselves up by the bootstraps and say, "I am OK. And I can be even better. And this is the way that I can get better." It may mean taking the drastic step of removing yourself from a particular environment. You may have to refuse to be drawn into certain conversations. It definitely requires monitoring your habits and behaviors. Again, ask yourself the question, what is important to me? That's where compassion begins.

When I traveled to Nashville in 2009, the question that came to me was, "What is important to me now?" And I looked at my father and I said to myself, "He is."

I had to develop tremendous compassion for both of us in order to be able to tell myself that truth.

Part of developing the compassion that can change your life is mustering up the courage to acknowledge the fact that the father figure is one of the most important figures in your life experience. Rather than trying to deny the importance of his presence, recognize your primal, basic need to connect with your father and allow the accompanying emotions to come forth.

When we deny or numb emotions, it's quite often an unconscious process. We may just say to ourselves, "Oh, I'm getting rid of that thought. I don't want to think about that anymore." But, as life lessons often do, whatever we try to stay away from keeps popping up in our experience. It becomes a nuisance. Every time the nuisance shows up in our awareness it becomes larger and larger in our minds. Then we begin thinking that in order to get rid of the nuisance, there has to be some kind of force involved, whether it is through verbal or physical means. If it all starts to feel like too much to handle, we may snap.

This is what happens on a personal level when people give in to the belief that they're not enough, when their self-worth whittles down to nothing. When a young man feels as if he's slid off into an abyss where he doesn't really matter, he becomes impervious to his worth and brilliance. Compassion is denied. The insensitivity and self-hatred that grows in a numbed heart makes it so that everything that looks like him begins to represent how he feels about himself. This is what happens to young men who want to get rid of other young brothers. They snap because they can't take it anymore and they end up taking someone else's life.

At the end of the day, they may not even know why they did it. Their conscious mind is telling them that they committed an act of violence over some tennis shoes. Or because someone else was getting comfortable in their territory. But all that is saying is that they numbed themselves to the point where they believed that nothing they do matters. They're worthless. And the other young men who look and talk and act and dress like them, and have had the same experiences are worthless too. This is an interesting way to tell the world that you believe in self-annihilation.

Allowing compassion to have full sway in your life is not to imply that negative things haven't happened. We're not letting someone else off the hook in that regard. It's that we allow the memory of whatever has happened to dissolve into the vision that I hold of what's important to me right now, which is the life of someone else.

Compassion is not feeling sorry for someone else. You can't have compassion for someone and feel sorry for him or her at the same time. I had compassion for my father because I loved him and I loved me and I wanted our relationship to be different. Feeling sorry takes us in the exact opposite direction in terms of action. We do nothing. To feel sorry for someone is, in essence, to give them the middle finger. I don't feel sorry for people. I bless people. I want to give those around me a blessing of power, one that undergirds everything else.

I speak my blessing to the part of the individual who wants to get better, because I've had the same compassion for myself. This allows me to see beyond what the eye of appearance shows me in regard to other people that I come into contact with.

I know there's a genius inside of you because I know that same essence of genius lives inside of me! That's the same energy that I know for my self because I've had to have compassion for my self as I grew into the understanding that I, too, am a genius. I, too, am OK. That truth, which is a spiritual, universal truth, can speak to you as well. It can speak to the core of your genius wherever you are right now. That's what I know!

Chapter 5

AWAKENING TO REALIZATION, REMEMBERING, REFRAMING AND REINVENTING

The Power of Surrender

When we think about waking up, we usually think in terms of waking from some kind of physical sleep. For our purposes, when we say awakening, we mean waking up from sleepwalking. It's an awakening of consciousness rather than a physical awakening. Conscious awakening happens on a soul-u-lar level when we begin to take a greater dive into our understanding. There's a shift that happens inside of us that is unparalleled to anything that's happening in the outside world. Awakening involves understanding how we fit into the scheme of what is unfolding on the planet. We become cognizant of the fact that we're participants of a global unfolding of history and human evolution, whether we realize it or not.

We awaken to our divine purpose here on the planet, asking ourselves the question, how do I fit in? Where is my place in what's happening? I see now that something is taking place far beyond what I can dissect with my natural eyes and my natural mind. There's something life-altering that is happening on another level and I'm choosing to wake up to that realization and play my part.

Awakening is closely aligned with change and transformation and shifting. It's like trying on a new mental suit. It also has to do with shedding. When we commit to the process of shedding (or surrendering) old ideas and perceptions, we give ourselves more room to fit into the new energy that's unfolding around us in our lives. Otherwise, we continue to live in a space that we've outgrown. That causes constriction on every area of our lives to the point where we literally feel like we cannot breathe. Refusing to let go of what no longer serves us keeps us from becoming conscious. There's no room to grow.

Normally, the friction that happens when a snake is about to shed it skin aids in the process; it has to have something to brush up against. This is normal. When we move into a shift in paradigm, the integration between the old ways we used to think and our new vision is part of the process of shedding the skin. It's how we step into our new perception, our new thought. That shedding will happen over and over again, at different intervals throughout our lives. Because the awakening process is just that: a process.

We are forever awakening to something that is bigger, greater, and more expansive than ourselves. We're a part of the whole. Most people live out the experience of separation. We're taught to believe that we're all separate from each other and that's fine because we can be separate and still get things done. Somewhere in our collective history we have chosen to believe that one group or one person has done it by him or herself. Whereas if we really take a good look at history, we see that a concerted effort by many different types of people have created the platforms for great successes to come about that benefit the whole.

We also can go back and look at history and see that one person may have spearheaded a great cause, but they had many people as followers and cohorts to bring the vision to life. If we're thinking that we can do life on our own, not recognizing that it takes the marshaling of everyone's resources to do that, then we've been mistaken. We've bought into the I/Me concept of living. What we want to do is awaken from the concept that we can do it all by ourselves. We must ask ourselves, where does the greatest courage and strength lie? It lies in numbers.

I've had to learn this lesson for myself. For so many years, I'd taken on an autocratic, self indulged, its all about me type of mentality. I valued independence instead of inter-dependence. But when we see that life is made easier and better by people coming together over a common goal, it behooves us to start asking ourselves questions like, where do I fit in? I had to surrender my ideas about having total independence in order to explore new ideas about the value of interdependence. I had an awakening to a new paradigm and, in order to embrace it, I had to surrender everything I thought I knew.

Just like the example about the snake shedding its skin, there's something that we have to let go in the process of surrender in order to embrace new levels of understanding in life. Most of the time it's not someone that we have to release, but rather our thoughts about someone or something. This can be difficult because in some instances, we've carried these thoughts around for years and years. But there are four steps that I want to talk about that can help guide us through the process of surrendering the old and embracing the new.

Realization

For most of us, we come to a point in our lives where we realize that we've been riding in circles on the same mental or emotional merry-go-round for far too long. I call this "the cycle of non-discerning good." Somehow we get caught up in the world of effects around us and we're not able to see past the fog. The discernment of what's real and what's not real becomes muddied. In the realization process, something, someone, or even a new thought will slow down the pace of the merry-go-round. When we slow down, the things that were only a blur before now take on definition and clarity. We can look at the pictures in our minds and see them for what they are, without allowing them to add to the tornado of mental chatter swirling around in our brain.

Then we can practice giving the new thought that's trying to get our attention the mental space to have its say. In order for that to happen, though, something else has to move out of the way. Something has to be released. We have to surrender to the thought of letting the old things go.

There are layers and layers and layers in the letting go process, just like there are layers and layers in the forgiveness process. The important part of the process of letting go is that we take the initial jump. In pertaining to the relationship with our fathers, we are being given the opportunity to reconcile the negative thoughts that we may have harbored. We get to remove our

fathers from the mental prison that we've held them in, perhaps
for years. We're now willing, in our minds and deep in our hearts,
to dig under years and layers of mental garbage to find the key
that will release them.

Remembering

Sometimes thoughts and feelings about the past can come
swirling at us so fast that it seems overwhelming. In that case, I
recommend two things. First, take a deep breath. Second, take
another deep breath.

This is how we take a conscious leap into saying right now
I'm going to slow my mind down. One way to do that is to get
centered, seated or standing, with your feet flat on the ground,
close your eyes and take a deep, cleansing breath. Becoming
conscious of the breath is a tool for centering and clarity that can
serve you for a lifetime. What happens when the chatter becomes
so overwhelming is that we literally forget that we're breathing.
We become like wind-up robots. The more we're stimulated—the
more that we see, hear, and do—the faster we go. But as soon
as we cut the stimulation off, we can stop ourselves and take to
look at what's trying to get our attention other than the outside
chatter.

The conscious breath calls forth surrender. They're like
brothers. One is on watch while the other one is on duty. When
we're breathing, we're quieting everything down so that the
thoughts and beliefs that need healing can rise to the surface of
our awareness. We can never grow until the memories and old

beliefs that need to come up from the heap of mental chatter into our awareness do so. This allows us to shine the light down on them so we can deal with them. Otherwise, they will just stay in the darkness, in the shadows, and continue to run our lives.

Surrendering the elements of our past that are holding us back is an ongoing life process. Self-discovery is a lifelong beautiful journey. And in the course of that journey, we're able to see things that we've never seen before. Surrender allows us to become clear on how to move through the seeming chaos and emotional upheaval that comes into everyone's life experience at some point. As we breathe, we find that we're able to let go easily and gracefully. You can't bring the old thoughts and beliefs with you as you cross over into new understanding. Something has to give. You can't bring the old patterns with you, because you've crossed over into a whole different realm of thought. But you must bring them up, remember them and honor them fully, in order for them to be neutralized.

This doesn't mean that, somewhere down the road, old fears and patterns and thoughts and beliefs won't try to grab hold of you again. But now you'll have tools that allow you to instruct yourself on how to move through that process.

Reframing

The voice of surrender speaks with a higher vocabulary. That new vocabulary gives us an opportunity to reframe past events with our current awareness. For example, think about the word pain. For most people, their minds travel back to something that has caused them pain in the past. We'll go back to a story, an incident, an occasion or an experience that caused tremendous turmoil. But when we reframe our past, we begin to look with new eyes at how the sting of pain manifested previously and how it may be different for us today.

The process of reframing is actually the process of taking something that has happened and allowing it to be reconstructed under a whole new set of mental codes. This type of mental coding comes from the awakening space inside us that's willing to be more graceful with how the incidents in our lives have instructed us. We can now reframe these incidents so that they become something other than the painful memories that they were before. Again, that's not to say that we're letting anything or anyone "off the hook" for their behaviors. But what we're doing is flipping the script. If we can take something and become mired in our thoughts about how painful it was, then it's possible to take the same thought and recode it by asking yourself, what was the lesson in it?

For example, my father's words often landed very hard, like a jumbo jet without a pilot. When I was about nine-years-old, my little league team went to the playoffs for the very first time. This was huge for me. Unfortunately, we were eliminated after the first game. When my father came to pick me up from the baseball game, my face was full of dust and you could see where I'd been crying because there were streaks all down my face through the dust.

My father looked at me and said, "Didn't win, did ya?"

All I could do was look at him and roll my eyes. What did you just say to me? I thought.

"No!" I said.

My father replied, "And you ain't gonna win all of them, cause you ain't supposed to. But the question is, did you do your best? Did you play your best game?"

Even in that little third or fourth grade mind, I stopped sulking long enough to think. And then I said, "Yes, I played my heart out."

My father said to me, "That's all that matters. Because you can't be somebody else's best. But you can be yours."

Then he started the car and drove off while I was still crying.

Years later, I'm finding that the real treasures in life come when you do your best. When you've done your best, you've won the game. In his way, my father was trying to get me to understand that winning and losing isn't all about a scoreboard. Winning and losing are terms of the heart. And when you've done your best in your heart, when you've satisfied your standard of excellence, then you have won. But I had to reframe that moment with my adult eyes to be able to capture its significance. It took me years to do that. For the longest time, I'd been too busy piling up unhappy moments to hold against my father in my mind.

I was too invested in the well-known, comfortable narrative about how mean my father was. Instances like the baseball playoffs happened all the time. For example, I'd come home and show my father my report card, which had straight A's. I was even a member of the national honor society. My father would glance at my report card, and his version of praise would be to tell me, "Yup, but if you keep hanging out with those hoodlums you gonna end up in juvenile detention and then all your little dreams are going to go down the drain."

How and why would someone say that to a young man who makes straight A's, somebody who is trying to be their best?

As I grew into adulthood, and I was able to look back at this experience, I realized that my father was trying to say, "Son, I see the genius in you. I see the brilliance in you. And I don't want anything or anybody to get in your way. I know you can do it. I believe in you, son." In the framing process, I awoke to this new way of seeing our interaction. I became aware that my father was expressing himself in the only way that he knew how.

My ability to reframe my time with my father started from the seed of compassion in my heart. Through the eyes of compassion, I became able to see that he was a human being. I also discovered that, through his lineage, he'd never learned the language to speak to me that I thought would land "properly." Compassion allowed me to put all eyes on my father and his experience, so that I could learn who he was and what experiences had shaped him.

Reinventing

When we reinvent ourselves, all we're doing is saying that there's more to us than meets the eye. We're more than we ever imagined ourselves to be. When we can say it and mean it, we step up to the place that Dr. Michael Beckwith calls "the leaping off point." It's the leaping off point to our greater good. This means that our lenses are now shifting. We're now seeing ourselves differently.

I learned that I was not just Charles the Football Player or Charles the Son or Charles the IBMer or Charles The Lion King Man. I began to ask myself, what else am I? Asking the question opened the door for new answers to bubble to the surface. Never in my life did I think I would ever write a book, much less two books. The permission that I was given when I said, I want to be a part of resolving the relationship between me and my father was the seed of compassion and reinvention. That seed of compassion said, you want to turn everything else around? I'll turn it all around! Let's change! Let's break the cycle! You said that you incarnated on planet earth to break the cycle that's been happening with the men in your lineage for generations. Well, I'll help you break every cycle possible. If you are here to be a vessel of divine good on the planet, you can continue to reinvent yourself and continue to reinvent every relationship that you have now. Because you started with your father.

The father and son relationship is a core relationship. The spiritual umbilical cord that connects father to son is there forever. We cannot get away from it. I tried to get away from it when I moved to New York, but it just got thicker.

I believe that we choose our parents. This belief manifested itself to me as I was in my own process of remembering, reframing and reinventing. I started thinking back to how tough my father was in my childhood and how he insisted upon me being my own person. The fabric of his character was grounded in this basic belief: be your own man. I began to notice how the treasures that he had provided for me growing up would surface to aid me in times of major challenge. Growing up, I had hated his counsel. But as an adult man, nothing proved more useful to me in becoming the person I wanted to be and living the life that I had chosen to live.

I remember when I tore my ACL (Anterior Cruciate Ligament) playing football in my sophomore year of college. I was on my hamster wheel, trying desperately to get back into shape to play. I was able to get back and even worked out for the NFL scouts. I had never worked so hard for something in my life. And do you know what my father said to me? He said, "You want to play professional football? You gon' get broke up, boy! There's some big ol' boys out there. You should want to take care of your body."

His words were gems. At the time, though, all I heard was, he don't want me to succeed! But what my father was truly saying was, it's more important to take care of what you have. I didn't get that connection until 2009, the year that I changed my entire diet, and began diligently searching for ways to take better physical, mental, emotional and spiritual care of myself. Only then was I able to reframe my father's concerns and understand what he was speaking from his heart. He wanted me to take care of my body for the future, because he knew what I had refused to consider: that sooner or later my football career would come to an end. But I would always have my self.

It was all a divine set up. I got everything I needed from my father one way or another. Even in moving to New York, he had already given me what I needed to be successful there. He had shown me how to be tough. My father had always told me, "You can't govern other people's lives. Govern your own life, if you can!" As a young man, all I heard in these words was a mean spirited challenge. But, once again, I found great meaning in his advice after the fact. In New York, I always wanted to correct the strangers around me for being rude, for knocking me out of the way or stepping on my feet or not saying thank you when I held open a door.

All of these behaviors were a major affront to my southern upbringing. But then I heard my father's voice. This time, his words taught me one of the biggest lessons I ever had in my life: we all have our own ways of moving through life. As long as you're not bothering anybody else, the world continues to function just right. When we start trying to put our ways of being and thinking onto other people, that's when we begin to muddy the waters. Then those muddy waters eventually become like quicksand and we find ourselves trying to survive in an atmosphere of judgment and mistrust and hurt feelings. Releasing the need to define or control others allows us to be free enough to see the people around us in a whole new light.

The Man

As the years passed and I grew older, I found that I wanted to know more about the man that I called father. I was finally able to accept the fact that perhaps I didn't know as much about him as I thought I did. I wanted to know more, to see him through a new lens. I was at a point in my life where I was more comfortable looking at myself. I also realized that furthering my self-discovery meant understanding my parents from an adult's perspective. My mother and I had always had a wonderful relationship. But my father was untapped. I hadn't spent a lot of personal time talking with him and getting to know him. There was something about his silence that made me inquisitive.

Perhaps the greatest character trait that my father possessed was that he was an extraordinary listener.

He said, "the way that a man speaks and what he talks about will tell you everything about him. Give a man five minutes to tell you about himself and he'll tell you everything."

I asked him, "Daddy, how do you know?"

He said, "One thing you find out about people is when you ask them a question about themselves, somewhere that gives them permission to open up to you. Because they find out that you have a vested interest in who they really are. The thing about it is that ya'll don't want to listen. You hear everything, because you turn your noise up so loud. But you don't want to listen."

My father only had an eleventh grade education, but he was brilliant.

Things finally came to a head for me one night when I was on tour. We were riding on a sleeper bus, trekking through Wyoming after a performance, of Jesus Christ Superstar, on our way to the west coast. I was exhausted and went immediately to my bunk to sleep after the show. After a couple of hours of rest I decided to go to the front of the bus and sit. Our bus driver was never without time to talk, so I engaged him. We began the conversation by talking about home and the places where we were raised.

"Do you know much about your ancestry," he asked.

"Well, my mother is a quarter Cherokee. I don't know that much about my father's side of the family, though," I replied.

"Well, my wife does a lot of research on all kinds of people and where they're from."

He went on to tell me that she'd made some really interesting findings based on facial features and shapes of body parts. I found what he was saying very interesting. I'd always been interested in the ancestry of my father. Dad and I had many similar facial characteristics. As a child, people's response to seeing me with my father would always be an immediate comment on how much I looked like him.

"Boy, you look like your daddy spit you out!"

As I grew older their words became grating. The suggestion that I looked like him at all became insulting to my ears. I'd always been interested in my lineage and what parts of the world my ancestors had traveled from, so I asked him if my features gave any idea of my ancestral footing. He took a few looks at me and immediately asked if my dad's people were ever settled in the Caribbean. I didn't have any idea if they had or not.

"Funny that you ask," I replied.

"People have always asked if I were from that part of the world."

"Your features, particularly the bone structure of your brow and your thin upper lip, resemble those of the Arawak Indian."

He continued on explaining how and why he had made the observation. As I listened, I made a slight turn with my head to take a look out of the window. A strange object blew parallel to the bus and after a few seconds, I finally figured out that it was a tumbleweed. I'd never seen one in person before. Suddenly, as I was watching the tumbleweed roll by, a vision of my father's face slipped into my focus. Startled, I quickly looked back inside the bus and returned to my conversation with the bus driver. But I still wanted to make sense of what I'd seen.

Slowly, I turned again toward the window and saw out of my periphery the same apparition making its way into full focus. I met my father's face. Right away, all of my past perceptions, conditioning and pains began to surface.

What are you doing here? I wondered silently. I thought I left you back in Nashville.

There was no response from the human-like face staring back at me. I took one last, hard stare into the soft eyes of the apparition before returning to my bunk to rest.

We had traveled hundreds of miles on our way to the west coast before stopping to get some needed food. As the driver settled into a parking space, the rest of the cast on the bus began rustling from a long sleep. I, on the other hand, was still restless from my encounter. I'd tried to sleep, but all I could do was toss and turn from one side to another. Every direction I turned I saw that face looking back at me. It never spoke a word, yet its focused gaze was more than unnerving.

That incident compelled me into discovering another side of my father that I'd not yet considered. The journey of uncovering who he was as a person and a man was one that I needed to undertake. I knew that being able to see my father as a man with a background and a history of his own to come to terms with would change my life, and our relationship, forever.

I decided to start by asking my mother some questions about my father. There were so many things I wanted to know about him: his favorite color, his favorite food, what he liked to do most, what made him happy, did he have a best friend? Ultimately I wanted to know what he thought about me. I desperately wanted to know his opinion of what he thought I was going to be when I grew up. The rest of my entire family seemed to have written my life's progress report and given me titles before I was old enough to crawl.

My most desired knowing, however was if my father loved me. That question had lingered with me for my entire life. I just wanted to hear him say it. One time would have been sufficient. I just wanted him to tell me that he loved me.

My father was a slight, but physically fit man. He stood six feet tall and maintained his weight at 175 pounds for the majority of his adult life. I wondered how he could eat so much food and stay as slim as he was. His plate would be piled with food at dinner. He could eat nearly anything he wanted and never gain a pound. He loved tomatoes, onions, and celery. I saw him on several occasions eat a tomato like an apple. Very seldom was he sick with a cold. He, to my recollection, never went to see a doctor until he was forced with severe back pain. This turned out to be the occasion of his diagnosis with renal disease.

He had a great smile and a healthy set of teeth. Never do I remember dad going for a visit to the dentist. He always used a toothpick after meals and a quick brush in the morning before he left for work. He was simple when it came to appearance. He never fancied designer clothing or accessories: a pair of durable pants and a long-sleeved shirt suited him just fine. Dad preferred to be warm even in the summer time. I don't think I ever saw him wear a pair of shorts or anything other than ankle high boots. He'd get dressed, slick his wavy hair back with Royal Crown hairdressing, and be on his way.

Although not a physically imposing man, dad had a way of

being intimidating. When he chose not to speak, his eyes were his way of communicating. He possessed a deliberate stare that could convey a full, clear message. When he did talk, I made sure I listened because it could be trouble down the road if I didn't heed his words. But the cadence of my father's voice was quite appealing to my ear. He talked with a slow, southern lilt. One that was distinct to that particular region, and characteristic to the men in his family.

Dad's tone, however, was his own unique trademark. Many of his explanations ended with, "you know what I mean?" He punctuated his words with hand gestures measured with strong inflections. Pauses in his sentences held within them enough space to grasp the essence of the morals and life lessons that hadn't been verbally articulated.

For a man who'd barely completed the eleventh grade, dad made good sense of his words. I believe his tour to Europe in World War II gave him literacy and "book" sense to grow on. But dad's forte was not necessarily in making sense of Einstein's theory on relativity. His specialty was listening. He loved to tell stories, and he loved listening to them, especially when they were personal.

"If you ever want to get someone's respect right off the bat, show 'em that you're interested in what they're saying. And if you ever want to know the character of a man, give him five minutes to talk and he'll tell you every thing about himself."

I can remember my father quizzing guests that came to our house. He would have a good old time with my brother and sister's friends. Dad would begin the conversation by asking a simple question like, "You from around here?" That was his way of getting the other person to open up and communicate.

"Always let people know that you're interested in who they are and where they're from. People love to talk about themselves," he'd advise.

I would sit, pretending to mind my own business, and listen to those conversations. I was certainly not the listener that dad was, but for a youngster I was pretty good at catching a message through a gesture or body language. I don't believe dad's intention was to meddle. However, I do believe his inquiries were deliberate. My father hardly ever smiled, so a boyish grin was always a sign that dad was not being sold on what the other person was saying. A big smile (one where you could see his teeth), on the other hand, meant that he was comfortable in talking with the other person. And if dad was inclined to share a personal anecdote, like one of his hunting stories, then you knew that our guest had passed dad's initial test.

Conversations with guests were one thing; communication with his own family was another. According to my mom, dad had a normal relationship with his father. She mentioned that for the most part they were civil toward one another. However, there were times that my grandfather would lash out at my dad with torrents of profane and demeaning words. The lack of affection, such as hugging and embracing one another, seemed normal as well. This was the code of conduct that he then passed down to me.

I remember my dad introducing me to his friends. I was taught at an early age that the way to show another man respect was to shake his hand – and not a flimsy shake, but a firm, manly gesture. I learned the impact of this social coding, as it became important in my personal growth as well as my relationships with others. The way you greeted others spoke volumes about what you thought about them, and more importantly what you thought about yourself. But I also wanted to know how do you show another man that you care about him. Was it okay to hug and embrace another man? Those were questions that I wondered about, and were often confused by.

My Father, The Person

For the majority of my life, I had only seen the two most obvious facets of my father: father and dad. To me, being a father meant that a man had the ability to conceive a child and, ideally, provide for and protect that child. Being a dad was everything else: having the ability to build a relationship based on love, connection, respect and involvement, among other things. I dissected my father in his roles as father and husband, sifting through my beliefs about his abilities with a fine-toothed comb. I then measured the "dad" part. All of my ideas were based on my thoughts and feelings of how these attributes should be fulfilled.

I recall once having a heated conversation with my brother about emotions where I mentioned how emotionally detached I thought dad was.

"No tears, no crying, no nothing!" I exclaimed.

"He doesn't have to show you any emotion. Think on the fact that you have a roof over your head, clothes to wear, and food to eat. Does that count for anything?" my brother rebutted.

"Sure, I have a roof over my head," I admitted. "But it would be nice if he could say, " I love you" to somebody sometimes."

"He does love you, can't you see that?"

"No!" I shouted. "But I'm glad you can!"

After a few hours of calming, my brother came to me. He was apologetic, but still firm.

"I'm trying to get you to see how hard the man has worked so that you could have a better life."

The man.

That was a revelation for me. My father was a man, too—a walking, talking person, just like me. He had feelings. He had emotions. He had a history. He had a story. And yes, he had a struggle. I had forgotten that he was a man with his own beginning. He'd been shaped by his childhood, adolescence, coming-of-age and manhood, history and his biography. This was compelling to me. I went on a hunt to find out more about this man who was father to three children, as well as a husband and who I had known as dad.

I'd viewed him through a one-dimensional prism for far too many years.

My Father's Story

My father, Clarence Nathaniel Holt, was born on February 20, 1925, to the late Robert and Wilhelmina Holt in a small black community called Lake Providence. The town had been named by a missionary who founded it in 1868. It was nestled in the southeastern corner of Nashville, Tennessee in Davidson County. By the time dad came along, the South was still as segregated as ever. Blacks lived on the rough side of the tracks, trying to be seen and respected as human beings with the same rights and privileges as everyone else. He had an older brother, John Robert Holt, who was like his twin. You never saw one without the other. The house they grew up in had four rooms: a front room that had a bed in it, a bedroom, a kitchen, and an accessory room where things were stored. There was no running water or bathroom. An old, weathered outhouse stood a few feet from the back door. They used a washboard to wash their clothes and a long clothesline to dry them. The roof was made of tin with three posts that held up a long wooden porch.

Dad smoked cigarettes and drank. Although he did not drink during the week, weekends were his days of freedom. He'd spend the entire Saturday with friends, often coming home to a wondering wife and eager children. I was particularly excited to see him, as a youngster. I'd wait up all night until he came home. He was always inebriated. But for some reason this made him more approachable and with less of an edge. I soon realized that hanging out with friends and drinking alcohol made for a habit that was no more than a coping mechanism.

He and my mother had two children three years apart, and then waited eleven more years before they had me. Raising children in a still segregated south was an intricate endeavor. Trying to navigate the dynamics of change, I imagine he often needed something to calm it all down. But everything had drastically changed by the time I came along.

I was the first generation born into a desegregated south. Opportunities have made life easier to manage in many ways. However, the residue of the past made it difficult for both my parents, especially my father, to see and believe that life was offering me a table of possibilities to choose from.

People usually were not in a rush in the south. They moseyed to the bank, strolled to school, and sauntered into the church house. Summers in the south were special. All of nature revealed herself in her full splendor, as we welcomed the season for shorts and t-shirts. In the summer, everything seemed to slow down even more. This could have been due to the weather. Nature seemed to take on the same lilt as its co-habitants. The summer storms slowly wafted in through a heavy band of soft clouds. After a day of sweltering heat, you could always count on a late afternoon downpour of rain. Fall and winter were also miraculous in their unique ways.

October was always crisp, as trees released their colorful leaves, trusting the natural order to reveal even brighter foliage the following season. Winters weren't too harsh in the south. There was never an over abundance of snow; however, an occasional ice storm could shut down the city for days. In its consistent flow, spring could be seen climbing up hills and high yards, dressed in lush green. Insects such as lightning bugs, ladybugs, and flying cockroaches were all in full flight in the spring - honeybees, sparrows, and dragonflies skating across shallow ponds and lakes; honeysuckle in full bloom made everything smell delightful. Life in the south could be frustrating, dangerous and heartbreaking, but it was also magical.

My dad was born a Baptist. Baseball was his favorite sport. The story told for decades was that he had an arm like a rocket and could hit a ball from here to eternity. But just like everything else, the impulse to dream was beaten out of him by the fact that being talented and black didn't count for much during that time. Unless you were an aspiring preacher, the prospects for success weren't promising. Needless to say, a heathen he wasn't, but neither did he profess to be a saint.

He was schooled in the Nashville Metropolitan School System. Trekking miles to the schoolhouse, he often mentioned how the needs at home would hold higher priority than book learning at a certain age. With only an eleventh grade education, he went to serve in World War II. He often talked about the poor treatment he and others received during the return to home soil. He made particular note to the appalling treatment of Black men.

"They treated us like dogs," he'd say.

I knew this was a terrible remembrance for him. He rarely if ever complained about anything. When he spoke of his coming-of-age as a man and American citizen his conversation would become fragmented. He seemed to relive the experience as he shared with me, often pausing as he recalled a particularly disdainful experience. After returning from war he worked as a male nurse at the Veterans Administration Hospital. His motto was: "When you get a good job you kept it as long as you can 'cause you don't know when and if you'd ever run upon another one."

Keeping with his rural roots, he had a pig farm in a neighboring community. He would come home from work and go immediately to tend to the hogs. I loved going with daddy to the pig farm. I'd jump in the back of his old Chevy truck, tasting the thickness of the summer wind through the narrow, winding country roads. He'd let me feed the hogs from time to time. Never was I allowed to go to the corner of the pen where the overprotective sow was. He stressed how aggressive they could be, especially if they were nursing piglets. He would often treat the pigs cruelly by taking his frustration out on them.

In my father's day, mentors were scarce and the only one to really share your deepest, most private feelings with was one's self. Not even the black Baptist minister could pry out any information. With this as the backdrop, I began to understand why my father and I clashed so hard for most of my life. That understanding opened a doorway to healing for me. Walking through that doorway was the most difficult, and most transformational thing I'd ever done in my life.

Chapter 6

THE INVITATION

The Power of Authentic Integrity

Whatever we need to continue on our divine path is right where we are. Regardless of the situation, condition, or circumstance, the true essence of what we are looking for is, simultaneously, seeking to support us in fulfilling our desire to be our best. This backing may manifest through a person, place, or unusual encounter. However, what It has undoubtedly come to help us reveal is the beauty and love that is innate in all living things to share, to receive, and to embody. Charles Holt

There are so many gems of discovery in the process of surrender that invite us to recognize and own the authentic power of our being. Nothing is sacred, not even our thoughts. Surrender invites us to give up any and all unhealthy thoughts about other people and other things and, especially, about ourselves as well. We dive into an ocean of loving-kindness where we embark on a treasure trip to find more new things to discover about ourselves. Inside that discovery lies our ability to become more familiar with our indwelling coding for greatness.

The greatness that we were all born to manifest can be activated by the conscious development of our character. There's a huge distinction between personality and character, though many people don't understand the difference. Personality can be swayed heavily by social coding, rather than our indwelling spiritual coding. It is often influenced by external expectations that have informed us on how we think we should act. Character, on the other hand, has to do with allowing ourselves to uncover the deep secrets of the inner voice that's always speaking.

When individuals become snared in the cult of personality that's so prevalent in our culture, they waste their time trying to create these vast, spectacular, magnetic personalities so that people will like them and so that they'll feel better about themselves. But character is the real filter that leads us into our own brilliance. So, whatever we come to understand about our authentic essence of who we are will not be shaken or confined by the limitations of our personality. We're not defined by our personality.

We come to know who we are through understanding the traits of our character. Most of the time, if not all of the time, our character is going to point to principles: integrity, dignity, peace, understanding, listening and compassion, among others. Those are the types of adjectives that we place under character. Personality may have a longer list of attributes, but what is sustained under the listing of character is far more monumental in terms of sustaining us throughout our lives. That's what we should be after: building our character, rather than developing a personality.

Up until recent years, I hadn't put great thought into the merits of my father's character. And as far as I was concerned, my father's (in my opinion) flawed personality had been the part of him that showed up front and center in our relationship to one another. My imagination had taken on a lopsided embellishment of facts; I was dedicated to defining my father a bad dad. Recognizing that I'd become stuck in my stuff, I took my baggage into a now reconcilable mind and a willing heart. As I laid it at the alter of my highest possibility, I chose, over and over again, to release the perceptions and certainties I'd carried for so many years. Of course, my surface mind had quite a disdainful rebuttal.

Why are you letting him off the hook?

You mean to tell me that you are going to pretend that none of this happened, like he did?

What a wuss you are!

But I knew that I would have to give up something to allow the new unfolding to take place. I wanted a healthy relationship with my father. However, that desire was at odds with the story I'd made up about him in my mind. At the core of my belief was a blame game. I wanted to make him wrong and I couldn't make him wrong without my story. The thought of him not acknowledging any of my hurts or complaints intensified my stand on locking him up forever. In spite of all of my dedicated inner work, there remained a part of me that showed no mercy and was willing to throw all the keys to freedom away.

The more I was able to reframe the events of my life, the more willing I became in accepting the tremendous blessings I'd received. As I talked about before, my father was never big on giving compliments. He was always looking at the other side of an experience. But rather than seeing him as hateful or even jealous, I have nothing but gratitude for his perspective. Much of what he shared is now a bed of wisdom for me to walk through and to embody. No, he wasn't so concerned if I won the baseball game. He wanted to know if I did my best. If we lost and I did my best, I did my best. That's the bedrock of excellence: learning how to do your best even if you don't "win." That was always his platform. I've simply grown enough to be able to mine the lessons from the experiences in ways that I was never able or willing to before.

When I showed my mother and grandmother my straight A report card, they'd make a big deal in exclaiming how proud they were and letting me know how smart I was. My father would say something like, "Are you sure you're giving your teacher enough time to explain your homework to you?" His comments were so far off the radar of what was presented to him in my mind. But he was much more concerned about my character, even ahead of my accomplishments. Hence one of his favorite sayings was, "a good name is better than gold. Nothing can define you like you have defined yourself."

My father wanted to bring my attention back to my essence, that which could sustain me over the course of a lifetime. In doing so, he shared himself with me in the only ways that he knew how. He'd never been schooled in certain nuances of communication. My father was a dark skinned man in the south, born the second son to a more charismatic older brother. At times, he probably thought, what have I been born into? He'd often say things like, "If you're black, get back" and laugh. But I could see in his eyes the pain that he carried. By the time he was able to say those words with a smile, he found some way to shuffle off some of the sting. What I'd never considered growing up was his journey, as a man, to find a way to speak his truth through that filter of pain.

Sometimes we're given roadmaps on how to pursue our journeys in life. But we're not necessarily taught how to navigate the paths when they turn muddy and treacherous. We get stuck and then we sink into our own gloom.

The world will never, ever give us a true perspective on who we are. It will always feed circumstance, conditions, situations and the past into the equation. As we commit to really understanding the character of our being, we are given the opportunity to embrace the fact that we're part of a whole. The thoughts of loneliness, fatherlessness and abandonment have one thing in common. They all put us into the action of separation. We may even want to be alone after a while because we think no one understands us. We become victims. We believe that we've been ostracized from the entire world based on how we feel about what one person says about us. In the process of becoming reinstated into a global social community, we have to come to some agreement that I do belong. And if I don't think I belong, I'm going to try to fit in one more time.

We also have to set it in our minds that we're not trying to fit into someone else's pocket or someone else's idea of us or someone else's cast of success. We have to mold ourselves into what we know we are. As we discussed previously, one of the best places to start is by agreeing that we're part of something much larger than ourselves. To get to that place isn't an easy take. If we have ostracized ourselves by mentally and emotionally setting ourselves apart, it's hard to get back to some semblance of understanding.

One way to re-assimilate yourself into the idea of your

own value is to become familiar with those things that already exemplify the character traits of success and inclusion: integrity, dignity, gratitude, healing, and creative genius. We can find them all around us, especially in nature. The consciousness that has been already set in motion, which extols us to be a beneficial presence on the planet, already understands that it exists in a vortex of inclusion. It's part of what we see every day and experience all the time in the virtue of nature. That's why exploring and contemplating nature is such an incredible way of becoming familiar with the eternal aspects of our own character.

The way that I began to understand the process was to first recognize that I had ostracized myself. After the recognition came the reconciliation; I began to look at the things that had been said and done to me in the past, and I asked myself, how is the sting different today than it was in years past? I was then able to become conscious of the fact that I'd grown in some aspect of my awareness and being. The next question that I asked was, how does this pain speak to the way that I feel and think about myself today?

Through querying ourselves, we once again bring to the surface the opportunity to look at what may be stopping us from moving on. We must also look to our own memories. Let us remember that the dreams we dreamed as children are actually still out there, waiting for us to catch up to them so that they can carry us through and over this extended sleep, where we feel separated and excluded. Somewhere inside of all of our questions is a spark that can get us back to a time when we had a greater impulse to dream.

We're being offered the invitation to release thoughts and

negative perceptions about others, as well as the hindrances to our growth that have accumulated under that entire train of thought. We're sweeping all of that away. We may create such a heap of mental debris that we have to continue periodically sweeping for the rest of our lives. As we sweep diligently, our minds become open enough to consider that there are other options to our thoughts about who and what we are now. And we must always continue to ask our questions, because we're forever changing.

Our targeted questioning primes us to be ready for a revolution. In my own process of awakening, I noticed just how convincing my thoughts about my father had become. These clotted thoughts had turned into more than opinions; they had offered an indoctrinated way of thinking and living my life. What I held devoutly in my mind was a system of embellished beliefs that ended up reaching far beyond the facts of my experience. The fact that my father had not come to see me play sports until my junior year in high school did not at all mean that he wasn't proud of me. His admonishing me to be in the house at a reasonable hour had nothing to do with him trying to take my privileges and freedom away. His verbal reprimands about the fate of me and my "posse" of friends was not at all a tantrum of jealousy. I had made it all up. The impulse for a fresh and new way of thinking was pulling me with a compelling power. Everywhere I turned, it was staring me directly in my face. I could not get away from it. Ultimately, it changed my life and created far-reaching blessings that I never could have imagined.

When I talk about my dad and the blessings he provided for me, sometimes I think about how things would've been different if I'd had the opposite experience. I wonder what would have happened if my father had been the kind of man to shower me with praise and accolades. Asking that question brought me to a realization. If, as a child, my father had told me that he believed I was a great baseball player and that he thought I could be a professional, I believe I would've spent the rest of my life trying to be a famous baseball player. Just because my daddy said it.

Now, being a professional baseball player wouldn't have been such a bad way to go. But what if I'd wanted to negotiate my own thoughts of what I wanted to be? When I look back now from my current perspective, when I contemplate how every step of my life was leading me to be where I am right now, I know that I must accept the invitation to celebrate all my experiences rather than condemn parts of them.

It's great when someone that you deem an authority figure or a mentor gives you recognition. But the other side to that powerful experience is about allowing people the space to find that kind of recognition on their own, within themselves. Imagine being in a play. We set the plot, so that the audience knows what's going on. But we don't want to give them too much information because part of the beauty of the play is allowing the audience room to use their imagination. It happens the same way in life. We want to give people the tools to achieve their dreams and goals, but we don't necessarily want to set their dreams and goals for them. There's a big difference. Keep in mind, that just like some children experience having an absentee parent, other children have the experience of being controlled or smothered by a parent. Both experiences have the power to be equally detrimental in different ways. We must chose to accept the gifts of our personal experiences, and leave the rest behind.

My father showed me the tough side of love. He demonstrated the things he believed I needed to know in order to make it in the world. He taught me how to listen. And as I've grown into adulthood I've learned how to listen and hear what's being said even under the tongue. I learned how to pull myself up by the bootstraps and say I am a great learner. I am a great student. I'm a great person. No one else can give that power to someone. Each of us must come to these realizations on our own. I was waiting for my father to say these things to me and he never did while I was a young man. What I received instead was the ability to find these truths for myself. The value in that is unparalleled.

The Invitation

During the last five days that I spent witnessing dad's transition, more than a few thoughts ran through my head. The only dad that I'd ever known in my life was about to be gone forever. Where did the time go? Our lives together played over and over like a movie, much of which was filled with tumult and misunderstanding. Scene after scene, year after year. As I watched the vivid images in my mind, emotions flooded my being; I went from sadness to disgust to anger to painful disappointment… and then to love. That road to love was the hardest most arduous stretch of the relationship, and it was worth every minute of it.

No matter how much time I spent weighting the spectrum of what I called bad, my resolve was always gratitude and love. What was I grateful for? I was more aware and awake than I'd ever been in my life. I had traveled through the hard streets of forgiveness. I'd cleared the path for wholeness and a new way of being with dad. So why was it so hard for me to push through this last stand.

Why are you dying on me now? I thought. It seems like we had just begun to have a friendship. Why are you choosing to leave me now after all the work we've done to get to this place?

The more I thought about it the angrier I became. I thought I had every right to be. Why couldn't I just be mad and leave it at that? Was there place for me to be pissed off at dad forever? But more importantly, why did I continue coming back to love when love seemed so absent the majority of the time we were together? But like always I was humbled by the mystery of life, which seems to tuck the answer inside the question.

Deep inside this experience was my figurative return to the altar. Standing before a host of witnesses were me and my father. Dad was firmly planted and ready to make his vow. He'd thought about the journey he so bravely made his way through and was ready for the one that he was about to embark upon. I on the other hand seemed nervous and unsure. I couldn't be still. My roaming mind had taken charge. My father's life seemed to speak from every corner of the room. This is what I heard:

"I, Clarence Nathaniel Holt, came to earth on February 20, 19 and 25. While I was here I vowed to do the very best that I could. I fell short sometimes, but I got back up and tried it again. In my heart, I tried to love everybody in my own way. Sometimes I got "like" and "love" mixed up, but I believe I got it right this time. And I never meant no bad things or wishes on anybody. I wanted to be the best father that I could be to my children and the best husband to my wife.

"There was no guidebook on how to raise a child or how to be a good spouse, so I attempted to write my own as I went along. Sometime I had to erase and adjust depending on which child I was with. I loved my parents with all my heart. They gave me as much as they could and I tried to give it to my family. I treasured my friends and I wanted to be the best friend to them. And son, I tried to love you with all I had. By the time you came along, things were different. Times were different. I was different. Sometimes I was a little scared about the "how's" and the "why's" but I kept doing the best that I knew how.

"There were things that I didn't say to you because I didn't know how. There were even times when my search for courage fell short. But it was in my heart. I loved you, son. So if you can do a little favor for me while you are still here I'd appreciate it. I want you to promise to do your best. Promise to give your best. Promise to be your very best. I know you can.

Love always, your dad"

The invitation was clear.

A Charge to Keep Forever

How could I resist? In the core of my being, I knew that this was a continuation of the work that I came to do and the beauty that I came to reveal and the flow of life I came to demonstrate.

I will, dad, I told him. I will.

One of the most complex days of a student's life is graduation from college. One of the happiest days for a parent is when their son or daughter graduates from college.

If a man doesn't take advantage of the opportunity to individuate from his father and reframe his past, he risks getting stuck. We're meant to be forever evolving. But sometimes we don't consciously evolve; we simply move faster on our little hamster wheel. One of the reasons that we continue to spin in circles in certain areas of our lives is that there are parts of us that haven't graduated. Our physical bodies grow steadily, but sometimes our mental capacities and the way that we govern ourselves in our hearts are still stuck in the past. They haven't caught up with the rest of us. When we act out negatively in relationships with others, at least part of our behavior is a demonstration or reflection of areas where we need to graduate into greater understanding and maturity.

If the patterns of our childhoods are never fully healed, we'll continue to act out these unresolved disappointments and wounds no matter what our age. When you don't graduate, your life eventually begins to unravel. As men, we must step up and demand better from ourselves and from each other. Excellence is about doing your best at all times. Integrity is about keeping your word no matter what. Equanimity is the grounds for self-respect, so that you can learn to respect others. When core principles like these aren't taught, passed down man to man, from father to son, or if we choose to bypass them, we leap into personality-driven tricks that we hope will help us get by.

After a while, our thoughts around pain concretize and we don't want to deal with them. So we hide out in our relationships. But when the relationships begin to spin out of control, if we're honest we can recognize that the debris that's surfacing is filled with past pain. When it resurfaces, if we still don't know how to deal with it we get caught in a vortex of personal chaos. People caught in a vortex of personal chaos literally do not know how to respond to challenges in a civil way. When we graduate, we still face a multitude of challenges in life. However, we have the wherewithal to stand on the bedrock of our character, taking on life's challenges and lessons in a civil, openhearted manner. In that way, we end the cycle of projecting or inflicting past pain onto others.

Some people aren't even aware that the pain that they project onto other people is made up of their own unresolved issues from the past. Another aspect of graduating from the past is taking responsibility for our unresolved issues. If we aren't exposed to civility and security and support and loving-kindness growing up, it can be a daunting journey to try to recreate that tapestry of goodness for ourselves in our adult life. But it can be done. That's where teachers come in to remind us that we have the tools inside of us to pull our lives back together. Then, at some point, we become the teachers for someone else. In this way we help to keep each other out of the vicious cycle of projection and acting out.

We're all being invited to live our best and highest good. Somewhere inside of us recognizes the different vibrational effects of the things we see demonstrated in the world. Even if we're inundated with chaos all of our lives, there's a part of us that knows and recognizes peace. We may not have had the visual demonstration of what peace looks like, but the impulse to be peace resides in each and every one of us.

There's no need to struggle to achieve these goals. Life gives us everything we need to wake up. After processing everything I'd experienced with my head and my heart, I concluded that the whole thing was a divine set up. A cosmic concoction by the universe itself, in honor of the sacred agreement I made even before I took on human form.

I asked for my relationship with my father. My creative genius knew that the only way to activate its seeds were through the tough and terrible times with my dad. Those times compelled me to ask questions and to seek answers from my own intuitive rebel. Dad's seeming faults gave me permission to stretch my imagination. In my quest to not be like him I became excited about the idea of learning to be my own drummer. He echoed that sentiment as well.

"Be your own man," he'd say. "Don't try and be like nobody else."

I'm sure that I agreed to be a beneficial presence and that I would add to the beauty, intelligence, and love that already existed before my arrival. Daddy's last few years gave me insight into the realm of ever expanding good—mine, his, and everybody else's. I watched him shed all the old ideas that had become attached and hardened in his surface mind—the mind that could only see through the lens of the senses and that, at many points, had been overloaded with information based on painful history. The staggering amount of negative data that he'd been forced to process had taken a toll, some of it becoming part of his way of believing.

He'd been a young colored (a word that my father's mother used) boy who grew up in a segregated south, struggling to find his place in the world around him. Then he was a young black man who held tight to a spinning world – managing his dignity and manhood through what could only be described as harrowing times. He became a father who wrote his book on family as he went along, trying to somehow make sense of the balance between responsibility and freedom. And then he became the old sage who decided that what he was and what he had given was all that he could offer. That was my dad.

One by one, he shuffled off the things, ideas, and beliefs that no longer served him in his new adventure. Faded into the light of his love were all the pain, the struggle and the misunderstandings. Dad, too, had a divine contract with himself to fulfill. Like me, somewhere inside he'd said, "yes" to a greater unfolding. However, I'm encouraged by my belief that dad knew that life could only get better and that he had a part to play in that truth. He was his best and gave the best that he had. Indeed, it was enough.

As we continue on our journey, the part of us that speaks to the essence and true nature of who we are will sooner or later have its say in our lives. Recognition of our true nature may only manifest after realizing all the ways we've seen the opposing nature of chaos being demonstrated in our lives. Sometimes what wants to come to and through us can only be germinated through a fire. The fire can be, I've had enough! I'm sick of this! What we're really saying there is, I want a change! I've been ready for a change for a long time!

Fire can germinate certain seeds that have been left latent and dormant for years. Those seeds can only become fruitful under a certain temperature. When that fire burns through and lights us up, we have the opportunity to say, you know what? It's time for the change to take place and I'm that change. I've got to move and if I say I want peace, I've got to be peace! Now, how do I become peace?

Now, you've stumbled upon the real question. At that point, you get to go on a treasure hunt with your own soul. Because peace is after you. Peace is courting you. It is waiting for you to become interested about the ways in which you're here to demonstrate peace on the planet. Peace, like all the other qualities of the spirit, is ultimately going to manifest through your relationship to others and to yourself. That's when you become visible and contagious—because you're heated now.

This is where you let go of the pains and expectations of the past and agree to be your best, now in the present. Being the best isn't competing against what someone else does. It's allowing the demonstrations by teachers and mentors to give us indications of how great we can be as well. We're not trying to duplicate what these great people have done. But we want to set a course and a curriculum for our own unfolding. That way, we become our best. We only have our own particular way of expressing.

The spiritual principles that govern the world, and our individual lives, all have a season and will bear fruit for us in good time if we will allow it. That's part of stepping into the energy of being our best. And most of us do strive to be our best without being consciously aware of it. But the power of consciousness is that we recognize those qualities of greatness because they become a part of how we continue to create them.

The world is calling for our best. The world isn't asking for the best of just one person. It's asking for the best in all of us, individuals in a collective thought.

Chapter 7

THE LEGACY

The Power of You

T here are private and public legacies. When we think of a legacy, we often think of people who've been noted for accomplishments or assets that they've bestowed upon society. But in some cases, a legacy could be breaking a cycle within your lineage that has been held for years. A legacy can mean freeing yourself from ways of being or patterns of living that have been handed down subconsciously through the generations. A legacy could also be becoming the first person in your family to go to college or graduate from high school.

The common denominator is that the point of legacy is where you become the living manifestation of something that has never been experienced before. The kind of spiritual legacy that we're talking about here has within it a quantum leap effect. You have to get past something that has existed for years to get to the other side. As you take that leap forward, you advance the possibility that the condition will never exist again in your personal or familial dynamic.

Legacy leaves a trail of demonstrations, showing us how to realize certain goals that haven't had the support of demonstration before. For example, a person could set out to learn Spanish in the hopes of creating a particular legacy within their family of being multi-lingual or, perhaps, traveling the world. Sometimes an emotional legacy is left for future generations. The descendants receive certain pointers from the wisdom that's been passed down, in order to further develop their own path as they move through the same type of journey. Someone who is the first in their family to graduate college might have the intention of starting a legacy where every child in the family receives the opportunity for higher education.

When we accomplish great things, we leave a trail of possibilities and examples for those coming behind us, that they may have a map and know what's possible in their own lives. A legacy is a grand example of how good and how successful one can be. Of course, there are also other types of legacies. Fatherlessness is a legacy in some families. But the thing about a true legacy is that it's always going to benefit generations to come. Fatherlessness is a condition that can be passed down through the generations. But it doesn't have any redeeming factors associated with it that would allow us to consider it a true legacy, in the terms that we're using to define it here. A true legacy uplifts others.

A legacy begins when an individual decides that he or she wants to break a cycle, or wants to have something of great value to pass along that will benefit those of their line in the future. They start a whole new grounding in soil that is rich enough to sustain a family or community in a new way. It stems from an individual's decision to pursue the opportunity for lasting change, because the old way of being is no longer an option.

We can also create our own personal legacies within

ourselves. We do this all the time when we change our minds and change the ways that we respond to the world. That is a legacy of emotional and spiritual evolution within itself. Then it becomes a demonstration. If we demonstrate the realization of possibility, we become contagious. Everybody wants to be like that. That's when it expands to a larger platform and then others want to be a part of it as well. In some cases, we call it celebrity or stardom. But it all started with someone's attempt to build a personal legacy.

Legacy begins in the funnel of self-discovery, where we understand that we're forever changing. As we change, we grow more and more into the truth of who we are. That truth gives us the platform to demonstrate those things that we've come to know about ourselves. As we continue to express our authentic truth, we become contagious agents of change and transformation. Because we're forever shifting, this consciousness of demonstration and discovery begins to infiltrate every place that we go. People want to be like us. They want to do the same things that we do. Legacy then turns into a platform to give other people permission to transform into their authentic good. It's like a big oak tree that continues to grow for centuries from one small acorn. Every branch has its own legacy, with the trunk of the tree as its center point.

The Geometry Lesson

My father left a legacy that will not only survive through his family, but through the thousands upon thousands of people who read my books and hear me speak or sing. Everyone that I encounter, no matter how briefly, will benefit from the lessons and the wisdom that he shared with me. But for most of my life, I didn't understand or see my father's contribution to my life as the fulfillment of a powerful legacy. Instead, our interaction felt more like a geometry lesson. Let me explain:

I was always a stellar math student. When I graduated from honors algebra, I was ready for my next mathematical adventure: Geometry.

But geometry, for some reason, didn't sit well with me. Maybe it was all of the acute angles and varying degrees that threw me off. All I remember was throwing my pencil up in disgust and frustration.

"I hate math," I cried! "It doesn't make sense."

It made sense all right. I just couldn't make it make sense to me. After sessions of pleading with my teacher, and refusing to believe that all of those right angles and dimensions were in fact adding up, I decided to stop pouting and give it a chance. After weeks of struggling and through incomprehensible problems, I finally stumbled onto a greater understanding of the subject. And, of course, the breakthrough came sports.

We were playing a cross-town rival in football. The game was on the line with us trailing by three with two minutes and thirty-two seconds left in the fourth quarter. Why we had struggled with scoring was perplexing to our entire offense. Just when a hole off the right tackle seemed to open, there would be a linebacker to plug it at the last minute. This riddle puzzled us the entire game. It didn't look like we'd ever get the break we needed to change the scoreboard in our favor, and it was now fourth down.

If we don't get the first down, they would get the ball back on downs with just enough time to run the clock out and win the game. But all we needed to secure another set of downs was four yards. It seemed an easy task—just four measly yards. I could do a standing leapfrog to a first down. But what seemed like it should be a walk in the park felt like running a gauntlet in our minds. All night we had struggled with making inches on critical downs. A hard fought battle had taken a toll on both teams. We were exhausted. However, the question remained: Could we do it? Well, of coarse we could. The real question was: Would we do it? The answer lied within our willingness.

Had we played to the best of our ability? Did we have more to give? How bad did we want it? And finally, what would it take for us to get to the first down marker? We huddled and our quarterback called a play to the short side of the field. I took a quick survey to my right and to my left side before the snap of the ball.

"Set 229… 229….set… hut, hut!"

I took the handoff and let my pulling guard lead me around the right corner. With one eye glued to my escort and the other eye on the marker, I felt the gap between me and the sideline rapidly closing. If I didn't make the distance in time, the game was over. I quickly realized that I needed to cut my angle shorter so that I could at least get a few more inches farther from the impeding tacklers. With a swift spin of the hip I made the adjustment that would give me a little more room to cut up field to what little daylight there was to run to. By the time we collided and landed to the ground in a pile, the football and my body had catapulted past the marker for the first down. We would eventually cross the goal line with seconds left on the clock and another hard earned victory.

During our team meeting our coach continued to replay the run that set us free. For some strange reason I could only see the intricate outlining of the play to the sideline, like the detail of a perfectly sketched out dotted line. Planes and perpendicular lines appeared in my mind of nowhere it seemed. It dawned on me that the "game of inches" was completely relevant to my course in angles. The angles that I had defiantly resisted in understanding in geometry class were the same angles that I saw played out in the game of football.

Although it was easier to watch than to process on paper, the connection was becoming clearer in my mind. It took the entire semester to reach excellence in geometry class, but I eventually did it. It was an accomplishment well worth the hard work and time. Like the nail biter of a game we had, geometry not only taught me how to work through tough times, but I became willing to find the value of something that I had written off as unimportant.

I don't think I ever really understood geometry like I understood algebra. But the fact that I could relate it to the sport I loved so much made it easier for me to try it on. Not to mention that in order for me to keep playing and to graduate, I had to find a way to pass the class. This was the biggest incentive for me to "hunker down" and put my brain and my skill to the test.

Most importantly, over time I was able to see that what I needed from those geometry lessons that semester paralleled my experience with my father. I never really understood him either, and I was trying to understand all of him. And although I never understood all of him, I got what I needed from him. Because algebra was so easy, when I bumped into geometry, I wanted to leave the class. But I couldn't because I'd been in there for two weeks and if you attended a class for an extended period of time, you couldn't leave the class early without a failing grade or an incomplete. So I was kind of stuck.

Somewhere along the line I chose my father, who I didn't understand, and then found myself stuck with him. I eventually realized that I was stuck with him because there was a lesson in that relationship that I needed, just like there were lessons inside the geometry class that I needed to get. The lesson called for many different resources to solve the problems. It was one that would need time to figure out. And just like geometry, after a while the course began to wear on me. But sometimes someone has to initiate the healing. Willingness can be revealed in the smallest glimpses. Nevertheless, that glimpse is the invitation into a brand new beginning for everyone involved.

Finally, the lesson from my experience with geometry that stuck with me the most revolved around how I relate to challenge. Geometry was all about these acute angles and things that didn't make a lot of sense to me. I tried to understand about acute angles by relating them to things my father had said to me that I really didn't understand. In coming to understand that I wasn't necessarily going to understand the significance of why it was called an acute angle, all I needed to know was that there was a formula behind that definition of an acute angle. So, in my relationship with my father, I didn't always understand why he said the things that he said. But later on in life, like I learned in geometry class, I understood that my father said the things he said because they meant something in the overall picture.

I couldn't change the nature of geometry. Early on in the semester, I wanted geometry to be like algebra. But it wasn't algebra; it was geometry. And I wanted to, perhaps, change my father from being so hard with me. But he wouldn't have been my father if I'd been able to change him. So, you take what you're given and you look at it for what it is. Certain things are really complex, so we're not going to get to the bottom, or the underlying definition all the time. But if we hang in there and persevere with what we've been given and we at least make a striking attempt to try and understand it, then it will reveal itself and how it can serve our unfolding.

Accepting things as they are serves your unfolding, which strengthens you. We're not made to understand every detail of every experience. What these lessons have come to give us is an indication to how life wants to show up and unfold through us. Basically what my father came to do was give me the tools and gifts that would allow me to continue to build my own legacy. In doing so, it didn't necessarily mean that I'd understand every word of what he said, why he said it at the time that he said it, or for what reason. All of those details become too complex after a while. But by hanging in there I eventually got to understand what was most important: the legacy inside of the experience.

When things happen in life that are unfortunate or uncomfortable, it's easy to say, "I don't want it!" It's also very easy to blame another for the state of our affairs. But if we really look at it and say, what are you all about and then stay in there with it, then the experience shall reveal what it's come into our existence to reveal. This is the gift of legacy; it pulls us back from the edge of defeat into a whole world of greater possibility.

Just like the football game was on the line, so was my relationship with my father. Likewise, when I looked at the situation from a different vantage point, I realized that what I saw in my mind as a wall, turned out to be something completely different. When I took the ball and started running, I saw an opening. The thing that I'd learned about geometry was that if you get to a certain point, an apex if you will, if you don't make a cut, then you will have gone beyond a 45-degree angle. If I'm running and the 45-degree angle is what I need to get the first down and I go past that, then I won't get the first down. Geometry taught me that if I trusted what I'd learned about the 45-degree angle in getting to, or getting past a certain point in my life, then I could get the first down and get another chance at breathing.

Staying available to something that you might otherwise write off or reject creates an opening. All walls have spaces in between them. We just can't see them. If given the right situation, the opening shall reveal itself. We must practice seeing past what the eye of appearances puts in front of us. This observation was a large part of what led me to call my father and forgive him. If I'd said in my mind, it's not going to do any good. It's like running into a brick wall, I would have stayed where I was in my life.

When we stop moving forward, we begin to perpetually see walls in our minds because of harsh words and experiences and pain and deep disappointments. One way to start moving through those walls is being persistently faithful to the person that you know yourself to be. If I hadn't had trust in my abilities, I probably would have said, "Coach I want to come out of the game. Put somebody else in there." But there was something in me that knew that something was going to have to give. Once I persevered and stayed in there, it did give. It moved. It shifted. It altered its state.

You allow the shift to happen, as well as make it happen, through participation. We must participate in our own unfolding. Otherwise, it's like saying that you want to be a great businessman, but then you never pick up the phone to make any type of business deals or arrangements. That's not participation. That's hope—hope that somebody will call you and bring your dream to life for you. But there has to be real participation, and most of the time we have to initiate that. We sometimes believe that when we initiate things, it requires that we push and struggle and scrap and scrape. And that is what some people experience. But participation, in its most powerful state, is allowing.

When you've done your best in creating an environment for things to transpire on your behalf, all you can do is wait and allow those things to manifest. If you push and you scratch, you're going to go against the very intention that you've set out to manifest. It's like being in battle with your self. Trying to push through a wall is one of the hardest things to do. But when you allow the wall to crumble, or to be altered in your mind then the energy begins to shift and find that you can walk straight through. This is a simple, (though not an easy) transition to make. But our lives can change completely once we learn to embrace our transitions, instead of battling them.

Transitioning

A couple of days after I arrived at my parents' home to visit back in 2009, my mother abruptly woke me.

"Go and see what's wrong with your dad," she said.

I quickly jumped out of bed and rushed to my father's room. He was sitting on the side of the bed, holding a box of Kleenex napkins.

"I want to see my mama!" he bellowed.

He kept repeating it over and over. I'd never seen my father in such dire straits before. He had very seldom expressed his emotions, and him crying was not common at all. Although he had openly begun to share his feelings, the urgency in his plea was stark.

"I've been dreaming about my mama. I can't get her off of my mind," he wept.

I stood still asking my inner guide what I was supposed to do or say. The reply was, nothing. Let him have his time to release. You stand there and give him all the love you have.

"It's alright daddy," I said.

He finally calmed down and I returned to bed. I could not go back to sleep after the encounter so I allowed it to continue resonating with and speaking to me. A few days after the experience with dad, I sat on the bed in a moment of silence. He's going to leave you soon. He is ready to move on, I heard. I wasn't ready for the clarity of those words. However, I believe dad had made clear his intent to begin his exit. Of course, I tried to figure out when all of this would take place. But that was part of the plan as well. Dad, in his own way would co-orchestrate his departure just like he did his arrival.

Change is scary, whether it's physical, emotional or any other sort of change. Most of the time, we create huge walls for ourselves, which then gives voice to thoughts like I don't know how I'm going to do this. I've never done this before. This is too big. I could never accomplish this. When we allow our divine self to lead the way, inside of that journey is a plethora of guidance, as well as tools that will break those Jericho walls down in our minds. Because that's where the walls are. There is no wall in front of us. There are only walls that we've created in our minds.

If we listen to the intuitive genius that we have inside of us, it will give us access to the tools to allow the walls to dissipate or dissolve or resolve into the nothingness from which they came. We do that by trusting that there's a way to move through what we're facing with ease and grace, rather than through struggle, and to be persistent with our belief. In the meantime, we're continuing to work on building our authentic self so when the door opens we're able to walk right through it to the next level of our greater unfolding.

When my father had that emotional outburst, he was allowing the walls to crumble. He was allowing the walls of social and cultural coding, which had caused an emotional stagnation in him for years, to dissolve. He rejected the code that insisted that men don't cry, and if they do they don't let their sons see them cry. Somewhere inside him knew that this was the way to the next step in his adventure. Letting go of the old codes would allow him to open the next door and step through to the other side.

My father finally went through the great transition, where he released the things of this world and moved on to the next.

But we're all transitioning. And we all have walls. Depending on where we are, the walls may look like the Great Wall of China in our minds. Yet and still, for the walls to come tumbling down, there has to be a release of what we've held onto as being the truth of who we are. The walls aren't walls themselves. They're representations of how we're surrounding ourselves with mental fortresses that no longer serve our evolution.

Between Me and.... Me

What I ultimately found out was that this path through forgiveness to freedom was more about myself than it ever was about my father. Inside of the journey from then until now were markers showing the growth in the relationship with him, but even more were the historic settings that I had achieved in my self. I often wonder what would've happened if I had not have called and forgiven my dad. What would have become of the relationship if I had chosen to throw away the key to reconciliation? Would I have been ok if he had never said I love you? I admit, even after I chose to speak my truth to my father by telling him that I loved him and managing to release the expectations of him responding with the same, a part of me held deeply to the possibility of him one day saying those words. And he eventually did. But the thought of him not saying it still lingers. Now that he has moved on, I wonder if I would have been ok if he hadn't. I don't know for sure, but I believe I would have eventually gotten there.

As much as my father's passing grieved me, I knew that it

was time; the body temple could not accompany my dad to the next stage of his unfolding. That which serves as a vehicle, our body temple, allows the spirit to reveal and demonstrate the face of its creator. In essence, the body becomes the spirit's escort. This makes the body a vital and necessary part of our journey here on earth. Mind, body, and spirit all work as one, for one without the function of the other is deficient. The mind is the part of us that's conscious and aware and it dictates what we do with our bodies. When thoughts are of low vibration or without clear intention, the mind is operating at its bare minimum. Never scraping beyond the surface or exterior appearance of our thoughts fosters a shallow experience with life. It creates a static, slow moving existence. Because the mind is settled in this particular way of thinking, the way we express those thoughts become manifest in our actions.

Once these ways of being become habitual, they tend to become concretized as part of our belief system. And once we believe something long enough, it becomes our own personal law. The belief has the power to govern our actions and affairs. An example would be the way that I believed that my father didn't like me and had it out for me. Part of my action was to not have anything to do with him and to keep my distance from him. The interesting thing was that I kept creating situations to make myself right about what I believed. When I heard the voice tell me to call him, I immediately assumed that I was supposed to tell my dad "I forgive you."

But shortly after I told my father that I was calling to tell him that I was forgiving him, I heard the voice admonish me tell him what you've been wanting to tell him for years. Tell him that. I knew what that was. When I finally told daddy that I loved him and that I had always loved him, I activated my dive into self discovery and with peace.

Lesson on Listening

Listening to the voice of wisdom within started me on a path to healing that changed my life and altered my relationship with my father forever. This seemed fitting because, as I mentioned before, my father taught me everything I knew about the value and the art of deep listening. Dad's legacy of love will live forever. I'm grateful that I had the opportunity to experience the arc of my father's life and allow the resolve of a tumultuous beginning to clear away the pain, misunderstanding, and harsh disappointment. What came to surface during that process wasn't always pleasant to look at, but it offered truth beyond the measure and scope of situation, conditions, history, and coding.

Listening, as it pertains to this point in our collective history, is one of the greatest universal tools that we can grab hold of. It seems like every single thing that comes into our awareness on a daily basis is trying to get our attention. And we're hearing all of it, but we're not really listening to what's being spoken underneath all of the chaos. If we were listening, we'd be doing things differently. We'd be treating ourselves, as well as others differently. We'd be promoting health and wholeness in our bodies and our relationships if we were listening. We wouldn't allow bills to be passed that constrict the rights and freedoms of our citizens if we were listening. Life wouldn't be all about me, me, me. It would be about us if we were listening. We'd be prioritizing forgiveness, reconciliation and peace of mind in our relationships with our fathers, looking and listening for the gems that we received from them and letting go of the rest.

Listening is the ability to extract the nuance of what's being spoken under the noise that we're hearing. Listening is an infinite type of vibration, in that it's going to continue to offer us a path to truth. The vital aspects of what's being spoken all around us come to the surface through the practice of deep listening.

Listening and hearing aren't the same thing. What we hear comes from all different angles. What we listen to is a funnel that focuses the information down to what's really being spoken. You can have ten people talking in a room and you can hear everything that they're saying. But what is it that any one of them is really trying to convey? That kind of information is found in the listening, where we also discover the universal principle of compassion.

If nothing else, my relationship with my dad held one of the most precious invitations that I could have ever been extended. All of my wishes to be great, all of the ways I wanted to exemplify excellence, all of the things that I wanted to accomplish, all of the great intentions I had for my work and ministry, and all of the good that I wanted to demonstrate and share with the world… is all wrapped up in all of the time I spent with my father. The invitation gave me permission to dive deeper into my understanding of who and what I am. I got to take a peek at the dynamic character that lies within.

The lessons that dad taught me gave me access to tools that would allow me to continue to uncover those gems of wisdom. His words–yes, those gnawing, irritating, agonizing words–remain poignant markings of promise, girded by wisdom and fortified by a depth of embodied truth. How wonderfully amazing! I couldn't have set it up any better. It's the same for all of us, even when it feels difficult if not impossible to see; our relationships with our fathers have given us gems to mine as we uncover the vast strength and power and perseverance of our character. Without those experiences, we wouldn't be the men we are today, with the ability to go forth and great amazing legacies of power and compassion for the generations to come.

Dad taught me how to find me. Rather than staying stuck in feelings of abandonment and anger, I've come to understand that he was instrumental in helping me to learn to navigate my own way.

"You don't have to hold your bat like everybody else does," he'd say. "Hold it your way."

I never would have had the courage to leave the south and make the journey to New York City if dad hadn't have given me a glimpse of what I could discover in my own world. There are so many things that I remember that my father said, that serve as roots, grounding me in the world. I wasn't able to understand them then, but now they are like fresh springs falling on to dry ground. I am finding greater strength in my relationships with others as a result of something he reminded me of through my selfishness: "Ain't nobody gonna give you nothing for free, you got to give something to make it work for everybody." Back then I couldn't be convinced that it wasn't all about me. I know better now.

When you release yourself from the constricting and

deafening thoughts about how you think life is, and embrace the truth of the human experience and how beautiful life can be, you can walk through a field of possibilities, choosing to see the good in yourself and others. This empowers you to become even better and stronger and more available and willing to share your gifts and your talents. Now, all of a sudden, you're finding those gifts and talents.

Now, you begin to sweep away the debris to find this cosmic shine called you. You've allowed yourself to create an environment where you can use all of your experiences to help you access more of your authentic voice. It's like you go on a deep-sea dive into self-discovery. You go further and further down until it becomes the most wonderful ride of your life. Life becomes exquisite. And, again, we're not talking about a world without challenges. And we're not saying that whatever relationship you may have with your father will miraculously change overnight. Rather, we're talking about reframing and reinventing and remembering that we came down here to be powerful agents of change and transformation, giving everybody around us the permission to do the same for themselves, including our fathers. In this way, we can offer the blessings that we've received on the journey of self-discovery back to them. That's part of the freedom. We're not trying to impose anything on anyone. We're just living our lives the way that we believe is best for us.

We can't not be the beacons of light that we were meant to be. In essence, what we come to understand is that we're here to give our light and our love to the world. We're here to help those who are depending on us to break the cycles of pain and disappointment created by interrupted relationships and misunderstandings. It doesn't matter how long it takes, even if it's at the end of our time here. Eventually, we must give way to the voice within that has the final say, and step purposefully into our own greatness.

A Poem to My Father

TOTEM KING

Speak to me oh King
My ears are ready and willing to listen
You stepped into nothingness and became great
In my eyes you are a King
You braved a world unknown and became an answered prayer
Even through the quest you became your own man.
And in your struggle
You gave others permission to find their own
A word spoken to keep the dream alive
Sown in a vine of thorns were blooms of wisdom for the ages

Tough at times, your heart spoke through a gesture
To give a hello to brighten somebody's day
Setting it all free, like the true adventurer you were
The surface mind could not comprehend
Until the change appeared
Manifested as flesh summonsed from the Beyond
I shall continue meeting you in the depths of my Mind and heart
I will hear with the eternal ear your teachings and guidance
And we shall commune now spirit to spirit
For this is our sacred love
Where I know the unspoken shall reveal Itself
My ears are now mature enough to listen to what is under the
tongue
My heart embraces your melody
I will see you in the trees and riding the waves in this ocean of
good
You shall stand tall forever, dad
At the foot of your stature are roots extending into eternity

Some, I understand, still twisted waiting to be loosened by a present forbearer
Releasing us all to our healing and greater good wherever we are
The bridge, standing in the gap for the call to freedom
My eyes have been uncovered from the false sheath of reality
I see now
I see you now
I see me now
And the two worlds, visible and invisible, shall be one
I know who you are, and you know all of me
And now WE all know.

Thank you, daddy.

I love you always,

Your son forever

My Father's Words of Wisdom

You ain't gonna win 'em all, because you can't win 'em all.
Evocation of Excellence: Doing my best at all times no matter
the outcome.
I learned that being aligned with an Intention meant that
my commitment to diligence encouraged a strong work
ethic, subsequently learning the importance of withholding
an expectation to outcome. As a virtue of wisdom, I began
creating a higher purpose and achievement in all of my
endeavors and sharing.

It's not what you get; it's what you take care of.
Suggestion of Gratitude: Honoring what you have and being
thankful for all of what you have been given... even if it seems
like little.

Nobody's gonna give you something when it's is your
responsibility to get it on your own.
Ambassador of Self-Discovery and Self Worth: Creating your
own path to self fulfillment, happiness, and success.

A good name is better than gold.
Dancing with Integrity: Learning to embody the principles of
life and being of high intention with my word, my thought,
and my deed so that not only my work, but how I demonstrate
through my work goes before me.

You be who you are, and let them be who they are.

Courtship with Character: Being led by the core truth of who and what I am and what I came to the planet to reveal, to demonstrate, and to give.

Ain't nobody gonna give you nothing for free, you got to give something to make it work for everybody.
Call to Consciousness: Nobody is responsible for your life and your success but you. And what you contribute and share is not just for you, but it serves the good of the whole.

Don't bring nothin' into this house that you can't take care of.
Ready for Responsibility: Taking time to think before doing something that may cause harsh consequence and an unnecessary burden to your well being and to the well being to those around you.

When you know how to do better, do it.
Living Life: Learning how to do better and how to be better... then pass it on to the next person.